Essential Guide to Becoming a Disciple

Eight Sessions for Mentoring and Discipleship

Greg Ogden

IVP Connect

An imprint of InterVarsity Press
Downers Grove, Illinois

InterVarsity Press
P.O. Box 1400, Downers Grove, IL 60515-1426
ivpress.com
email@ivpress.com

InterVarsity Press® is the book-publishing division of InterVarsity Christian Fellowship/USA®, a movement of students and faculty active on campus at hundreds of universities, colleges and schools of nursing in the United States of America, and a member movement of the International Fellowship of Evangelical Students. For information about local and regional activities, visit intervarsity.org.

While any stories in this book are true, some names and identifying information may have been changed to protect the privacy of individuals.

Cover design: Cindy Kiple
Interior design: Jeanna Wiggins
Images: green grapes: Thomas J Peterson/Getty Images
      theater masks: ©goce/iStockphoto
      magnifying glass: ©Alex Belomlinsky/iStockphoto
      dove illustration: ©Alex Belomlinsky/iStockphoto
      sporting symbols: ©Aaltazar/iStockphoto
      gesture icons: ©-VICTOR-/iStockphoto
      hand icons: ©-VICTOR-/iStockphoto

ISBN 978-0-8308-1149-6 (print)
ISBN 978-0-8308-9322-5 (digital)

Printed in the United States of America ♾

InterVarsity Press is committed to ecological stewardship and to the conservation of natural resources in all our operations. This book was printed using sustainably sourced paper.

Library of Congress Cataloging-in-Publication Data
Names: Ogden, Greg, author.
Title: Essential guide to becoming a disciple : eight sessions for mentoring
   and discipleship / Greg Ogden.
Description: Downers Grove : InterVarsity Press, 2016.
Identifiers: LCCN 2016038019 (print) | LCCN 2016039657 (ebook) | ISBN
   9780830811496 (pbk. : alk. paper) | ISBN 9780830893225 (eBook)
Subjects: LCSH: Spiritual formation--Biblical teaching. | Spiritual
   formation--Textbooks. | Discipling (Christianity)--Biblical teaching. |
   Discipling (Christianity)--Textbooks. | Mentoring--Biblical teaching. |
   Mentoring--Religious aspects--Christianity--Textbooks.
Classification: LCC BV4511 .O335 2016 (print) | LCC BV4511 (ebook) | DDC
   248.4--dc23
LC record available at https://lccn.loc.gov/2016038019

| P | 20 | 19 | 18 | 17 | 16 | 15 | 14 | 13 | 12 | 11 | 10 | 9 | 8 | 7 | 6 | 5 | 4 | 3 |
| Y | 34 | 33 | 32 | 31 | 30 | 29 | 28 | 27 | 26 | 25 | 24 | 23 | 22 | 21 | 20 | 19 | 18 |

Contents

A Word from the Author

What motivated this study? For the past thirty years I have been meeting with men in small groups of three or four for the express purpose of growing together as faithful followers of Christ. Of all the responsibilities that I have carried as a pastor, nothing has been more satisfying than the life shared in these groups. After our time together I have consistently said to myself, "What an honor it is to share the joys and challenges in these men's lives. Where else would we have the freedom to be as real as we were today?"

My underlying motivation for creating these groups was to address the persistent need I had observed. Jesus painted a verbal picture about the importance of a solid foundation when he said that houses built upon rock can withstand the stormy times, whereas houses built upon sand are washed away (Matthew 7:24-27). Jesus is the rock on which to build our lives, but as I have walked with people in these groups I have witnessed the cracks and missing building blocks in their foundation. Even as my concern to help others build their lives on Jesus grew, I realized that I did not have a building plan. I was constantly scrambling to cobble together various resources to address different issues. To fill in the gaps I wrote *Discipleship Essentials: A Guide to Building Your Life in Christ*. This was my attempt to cover a broad spectrum of what makes up the underpinnings of the Christian life.

Yet I still had the nagging sense that something more was needed. As I looked at the Christian community through the lens of my pastoral leadership, I saw so many people who said they were

Christians but were not defined by that label. Many of these people had made a profession of faith in Christ that was meaningful to them, but being a disciple of Jesus was not their identity.

I wondered how we could engage those who have received the benefits of forgiveness in Christ to consider what it actually means to follow him. What if there was an on-ramp that clarifies what Jesus expects of his followers? What if there was a short study that helped more people to consider Jesus as their lifelong mentor and Lord?

It dawned on me that the Great Commission, given by Jesus to the apostles (Matthew 28:18-20), was not just the trumpet call for evangelism but also contained the answers to my questions. This short study of eight sessions is designed to be that on-ramp to a journey of following Jesus Christ all of our days. Once the decision is made to identify ourselves as his disciples, then we can go on to lay the foundational building blocks of a life in Christ.

Introduction

What Does Jesus Expect
of His Followers?

What exactly does it mean to be a disciple of Jesus? What am I committing myself to if I say I want to follow him? What will be required of me if I identify myself with Jesus?

These are the questions at the heart of these sessions. I believe Jesus himself would affirm that if we are considering becoming his disciples, then these are the kinds of questions we should be asking. Jesus says, "Suppose one of you wants to build a tower. Won't you first sit down and estimate the cost to see if you have enough money to complete it? For if you lay the foundation and are not able to finish it, everyone who sees it will ridicule you, saying, 'This person began to build and wasn't able to finish'" (Luke 14:28-30). Jesus wants us to count the cost up front because he is not looking for half-hearted followers who can't complete what they have started.

Francis Chan captures this half-hearted attitude with more than a touch of sarcasm. He invites us to imagine Jesus walking up to the disciples and saying, "Hey, would you guys mind identifying yourselves with Me in some way? Don't worry, I don't actually care if you do anything I do or change your lifestyle at all. I'm just looking for people who are willing to say they believe in Me and call themselves Christians."[1]

Of course, we can't imagine Jesus ever being this wishy-washy. Jesus didn't start a movement that has penetrated almost every part of the globe over the last two thousand years without asking for the ultimate loyalty of his followers. But what does this loyalty to Jesus actually look like?

Jesus has not left us with a muddle of vagaries. He gathered the eleven disciples together on a mountain in Galilee after his resurrection and delivered what we have come to call the Great Commission. These were their marching orders:

> Then Jesus came to them and said, "All authority in heaven and on earth has been given to me. Therefore *go* and make disciples of all nations, *baptizing* them in the name of the Father and of the Son and of the Holy Spirit, and *teaching* them to obey everything I have commanded you. And surely I am with you always, to the very end of the age." (Matthew 28:18-20)[2]

These three verses will be the basis for exploring the mission to make disciples, as well as the core characteristics that identify us as his followers.

Though the heart of the Great Commission is to make disciples, it also contains Jesus' thumbnail of what he expects of those who respond to his call to follow him. As you work through these three verses a phrase at time, a picture will emerge of Jesus' claim upon your life.

Getting the Most Out of *Essential Guide to Becoming a Disciple*

By following these suggested steps, you will be able to launch a network of on-ramp groups. The goal upon completion of these eight studies is that participants can make an informed commitment to become disciples of Jesus Christ. This lays the groundwork for a longer-term investment of building a sure foundation.

Make the invitation for others to join. Each group should be birthed in prayer. The facilitator prayerfully asks the Lord to draw him or her to those interested in considering what it means to be a Christ follower. The facilitator will then meet privately with individuals to extend an invitation that could sound something like this: "Would you join me and one or two others as we journey together to explore what it means to be a follower of Jesus? We will meet weekly to cover eight sessions over a period of approximately twelve to sixteen weeks. At the conclusion, we will then decide if we want to go on together to explore more about what it means to be a Christ follower."

Keep the group small. There are two main reasons that the ideal size of a group is three to four people: First, in order for real growth to occur it requires an atmosphere of openhearted trust, which can occur only in smaller units. The larger the group the harder it is to achieve relational transparency. Second, smaller units allow everyone the opportunity to share their thoughts and insights.

Make a covenant. In order to make sure there is shared investment, a covenant has been included that states the mutual expectations in the relationship. If you start a group with clarity and shared commitment, then it is far more likely to remain strong throughout your time together. As a part of the invitation to join the group, facilitators should talk through each item in the covenant, look through the table of contents and review the three-part structure of each session so that participants have a good feel for the amount of time required.

Find a private place to meet. In order to create the kind of trust described above you will usually need a place where others are not listening in. Though it is quite common to meet in public spaces such as a coffee shop or restaurant, the participants might be too self-conscious to be as honest or open as you are longing for in these settings. Spaces such as an office board room, home, church or even a quiet separate nook in a restaurant are best to foster the desired results.

Follow the pattern in the curriculum. Each session has three parts and is intended to serve as a guide for the discussion:

Core Truth: The core truth serves as the foundation on which each session is built. The rest of the chapter is designed to further clarify this central focus. Each session begins with interactive questions that are designed to bring out the meaning of the Core Truth.

Inductive Bible Study: An inductive study uses questions to explore the meaning of Scripture and set up a conversation with the material. Think of yourself as a reporter assigned to cover a story, asking the who, what, where, when, why and how questions. People complete their own answers to these questions independently and then share their responses as you work through the guide together. Some questions are simply *observation*, stating what is in the Scripture text; other questions ask for an *interpretation* of the meaning or conclusions that are implied from the Scripture; still other questions focus on *application*, applying the truth to where you are in life now.

Reading: The third element in each session is an article intended to provide a contemporary discussion of the core truth that will stimulate your thinking and challenge your lifestyle. Each reading has a study guide that will serve as the basis for your discussion.

Suggested format. Here is a simple way to divide up your time if you meet for ninety minutes:

Part 1 (30 minutes): *Relationship building.* Stay in touch with what is happening in each other's lives. At the start of your new group begin your time with some fun questions to get acquainted. Given that there may be a little anxiety as you get going, begin with something light that could foster laughter and create a sense of ease. In the subsequent weeks, follow up on prayer requests and what is developing in their lives. Go around the circle and ask if there are any joys or concerns to share together.

Part 2 (60 minutes): *Walk through the study material.* Do not feel the obligation to complete a session a week—just resume where you left off the week before. Get as far as you can and then simply say, "We will pick it up here next week." It is important to only go at the speed where you can comfortably interact over the content with appropriate application. This allows the relationships to remain primary.

You may also want to recite this prayer together as you begin:

Dear Lord, we are here together to listen to what you expect of us as your followers. Give us the courage to explore the implications of what it means to be your disciples. May this group become a place of safety and deep caring for one another. In Jesus' name, Amen.

May the Lord bless your journey into understanding what it means to follow Jesus more fully.

---

[1]Francis Chan with Mark Beuving, *Multiply: Disciples Making Disciples* (Colorado Springs, CO: David C. Cook, 2012), 17.
[2]Emphasis mine.

A Covenant of Commitment

The purpose of a shared covenant is to state clearly and up front the expectations in your relationship with each other. As you begin, review the following covenantal elements and share with each other in your own words your understanding of the commitment you are being asked to make.

1. I will complete the sessions prior to each of our meetings by answering all the questions as best I can.

2. I will make every effort to be present for all of our sessions in order to complete the entire study.

3. I will keep strict confidence so that whatever is shared in the group stays in the group without exception.

4. I will adopt an attitude of exploration and be open to considering the varied dimensions of Christ's call on my life to be his disciple, no matter where that takes me or whatever that means.

5. Once I have completed this study, I will consider making a commitment to go on to a more in-depth exploration of the implications of what it means to be a fully devoted follower of Christ by engaging in the relational study of *Discipleship Essentials* and/or *The Essential Commandment*. (In this next phase you will gain a more complete understanding of what it means to be a disciple, as well as be trained to take the lead in discipling others.)

In the presence of my partners, I commit myself to complete the *Essential Guide to Becoming a Disciple* by fulfilling the above covenant.

Signed _____

Dated _____

1 / Jesus
Who Does He Think He Is?

LOOKING AHEAD

CORE TRUTH VERSE: "Then Jesus came to them and said, 'All authority in heaven and on earth has been given to me.'" (Matthew 28:18)
BIBLE STUDY: Mark 8:27-30
READING: Jesus, the Unrivaled Ruler of the Universe

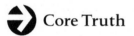 Core Truth

What authority does Jesus claim for himself?

Jesus declares the most astonishing thing that anyone could say about oneself: he announces that his Father has given him all authority over the entire universe. Abraham Kuyper succinctly and famously said, "There is not a square inch in the whole domain of our human existence over which Christ, who is sovereign over all, does not cry, 'Mine!'"[1]

• What key thoughts from the Core Truth stand out to you and why?

• What questions or issues does the Core Truth raise for you?

Inductive Bible Study

Since the disciples had observed Jesus heal, forgive sin, still storms and cast out demons for two years, the question of Jesus' identity had been on their minds. Yet it was Jesus who asked them the question "Who do you say I am?" *Read Mark 8:27-30.*

1. Jesus first engaged the disciples with the general question, "Who do people say I am?" How did the general public seem to view Jesus?

2. Why do you think Jesus asked the disciples about "the buzz on the streets" before putting the question directly to them?

3. What are some of the different views people have of Jesus today?

4. Think about the different responses to this question about Jesus' identity. What's the significance of these different answers? Why is the identity of Jesus so crucial?

5. Then Jesus turned the question on his own followers: "Who do you say I am?" Peter, speaking for the twelve, answered, "You are the Messiah (the Christ)." In Matthew, Peter's response adds,

"the Son of the living God" (Matthew 16:16). What is it that
Peter has grasped about Jesus?

6. By calling the question to his followers, Jesus raises the same
question for us: Who do you say that Jesus is?

Reading: Jesus, the Unrivaled Ruler of the Universe

The late journalist Sydney J. Harris was asked a discerning question
by a parent regarding the authority of teachers: "How is it that some
teachers are able to control their classes with a very light rein, and
have no disciplinary troubles, while others must shout and plead
and threaten and still get nowhere with the troublemakers?"

Harris replied that the authority of a teacher has far less to do with
teaching techniques or lesson plans, but with the "authenticity" of
the teacher. Genuine authority is the result of the "realness, presence,
aura, that can impress and influence even a six-year old. . . . A person
is either himself or not himself; is either rooted in his existence, or
is a fabrication; has either found his humanhood or is still playing
with masks and roles and status symbols. Only an authentic person
can evoke a good response in the core of another person."[2]

The most authentic person who ever lived was Jesus Christ. From
the outset Jesus impressed people with his innate authority. Early
in his public ministry, Jesus entered the synagogue on the Sabbath

and began to teach. "The people were amazed at his teaching, because he taught them as one who had authority, not as the teachers of the law" (Mark 1:22). Jesus then proceeded to deliver a man possessed by an evil spirit. Then they were really impressed. "The people were all so amazed that they asked each other, 'What is this? A new teaching—and with authority!'" (Mark 1:27).

The authority of Jesus left people shocked and spellbound—*amazed*.

WHO IS THIS MAN?

The Gospel writers contrast Jesus' teaching with that of the Jewish scribes. "He taught them as one who had authority, not as the teachers of the law" (Mark 1:22). The scribes, or "teachers of the law," were the scholars of the day. They had catalogued all the various oral interpretations and applications of the Old Testament law. It was their lifelong vocation to be walking databases reciting chapter and verse. The scribes would never render a teaching without a precedent from a well-attested source.

Along comes Jesus without any of the credentials we would associate with worldly authority. Under what rabbi had Jesus studied? From what school had Jesus obtained his credentials? What powerful office did Jesus occupy? Jesus made no reference to precedence. In his teaching he only quoted Scripture, not some famous and well-attested scribe. And when correcting distorted teaching, he claimed himself as the authority, "You have heard it said . . . but *I* tell you" (see Matthew 5:21-48, emphasis mine). Authority simply flowed from his being so his words struck the crowds as authentic and true.

Jesus grew up in a humble family in Nazareth and learned the trade of a carpenter. He seemed so normal, yet woven into the fabric of his ministry were self-acclamations and expressions of deity. Some have seriously argued that Jesus did not have a divine self-awareness. In the introduction to *The Case for Faith,* Lee Strobel recounts an interview with Charles Templeton, an early protégé and colleague of Billy Graham. Templeton parted company with the great evangelist in the late 1940s because doubts undermined his faith. Near the end of his life when Strobel asked him whether Jesus thought of himself as God, Templeton shook his head, "That would have been the last thought that would have entered his mind."[3]

On the contrary, the New Testament seems to raise this question on almost every page, *"Who does Jesus think he is anyway, God or something?"* Let's do a quick survey of Jesus' God-consciousness and authority.

Jesus functioned as Creator and Redeemer. His words accomplish what he commands.

- Jesus **commanded** and **demons obeyed.** He silenced an unclean spirit in the synagogue, delivered the Gerasene demoniac from his crazed condition and called out a spirit that had been destroying a boy's life (Mark 1:21-28; 5:1-17; 9:17-27).

- Jesus **healed** simply by touch or command. He rid a person of leprosy, restored a withered hand, stopped the flow of blood in a helpless woman and brought recovery of sight to the blind (Mark 1:40-45; 3:1-7; 5:25-34; John 9:1-25).

- Jesus **raised the dead.** Jairus's daughter, a widow's son and Lazarus were all brought back to life (Mark 5:21-24, 35-43; Luke 7:11-16; John 11:41-44).

- Jesus **ruled over nature.** Jesus walked on water, stilled a storm at the word of his command and orchestrated the greatest catch of fish Peter could have ever imagined (Matthew 14:22-33; Mark 4:35-41; Luke 5:1-11).

Jesus forgave sins. To the paralytic being lowered through the roof by his four friends, Jesus declared, "Son, your sins are forgiven." The scribes present immediately recognized this as an act that usurps God's authority for they thought to themselves, "Who can forgive sins but God alone?" (Mark 2:3-7).

Jesus asked for total allegiance from his followers. When Jesus claimed the new vocation for Peter, James and John—fishing for people—they left *everything* and followed him (Luke 5:10-11).

Jesus said that he had been given the right to grant eternal life (Matthew 11:27; John 1:12; 5:26-30; 17:2-3). When the disciples heard Jesus claim this authority, they weren't shocked nor surprised. The Greek word for authority that Jesus uses is *exousia*. *Ex* means "out of" and *ousia* means "being or substance." Put together, we learn that Jesus' authority flowed out of his being or substance. So when Jesus claimed "all authority in heaven and on earth" as he commissioned the disciples (Matthew 28:18), he was making explicit what they had observed throughout his ministry.

None other than Bono, U2's lead singer, pulls it together for us. An interviewer questioned his assertion about Christ, "Christ has his rank among the world's great thinkers, but Son of God, isn't that far-fetched?" Bono replied:

> No. It's not far-fetched to me. Look, the secular response to the Christ story always goes like this: he was a great prophet, obviously an interesting guy, he had a lot to say along the lines of other great prophets, be they Elijah, Mohammad, Buddha, or Confucius. Christ says, "No. I'm not saying I'm a teacher, don't call me a teacher. I'm not saying I am a prophet. I'm saying: 'I'm the Messiah.' I'm saying: 'I am God incarnate.'" . . . At this point, everyone starts staring at their shoes and says: Oh my God, he's gonna keep saying this. So what you're left with is: either Christ was who He said He was—the Messiah—or a complete nutcase. . . . The idea that the entire course of civilization for over half of the globe could have its fate changed and turned upside-down by a nutcase, for me, that's far-fetched.[4]

Jesus' authority is convincing because the prerogatives he claims, the powers he displays and the love he evidences are all integrated into the healthiest personality who ever lived.

As we have noted, Jesus' claim to ultimate authority is the intended backdrop against which the Great Commission is to be carried out. Jesus connects his authority to our marching orders with the word *therefore*. "Therefore go and make disciples of all nations" (Matthew 28:19). It is as if Jesus is saying, "With all the authority vested in me, I now authorize you to go." Jesus didn't just tell us who he is so that we can include it in a doctrinal statement that we recite in worship only to go and live our lives as we wish. No, he has a job for us to do and we have his full backing to do it.

THE IMPACT OF JESUS' AUTHORITY

Let's explore two implications of Jesus' authority in relationship to the Great Commission:

Jesus expects obedience. The first reason Jesus declares his all-encompassing authority is because he is to be obeyed. Jesus held up the example of a Roman centurion, a commander of one hundred foot soldiers, to teach us the implications of authority. This highly respected commander sent word to Jesus through intermediaries that his beloved servant was ill unto death. Before Jesus could arrive at the centurion's home he sent messengers to intercept Jesus, saying he was not worthy to have this healer come under his roof. The centurion understood how authority works:

> "But say the word, and my servant will be healed. For I myself am a man under authority, with soldiers under me. I tell this one, 'Go,' and he goes; that one, 'Come,' and he comes. I say to my servant, 'Do this,' and he does it."
>
> When Jesus heard this, he was amazed at him, and turning to the crowd following him, he said, "I tell you. I have not

found such great faith even in Israel." Then the men who had been sent returned to the house and found the servant well. (Luke 7:7-10)

The centurion was a man under authority; he took orders and gave them. But Jesus' authority exceeded anything he had ever seen in the Roman Empire.

Yet, could there be anything more contrary to the spirit of Western culture than the centurion's understanding of authority? The Western culture is proudly rooted in radical individualism. The prevailing attitude is, "No one tells me what to do or believe." We each keep our own counsel. This spirit is undergirded by relativism, the philosophy that all truth is relative to the person: "You have your truth about life and faith, and I have mine." Relativism says there is no single truth to which we are all accountable. There is only individual, personal truth.

But along comes Jesus who says that he is a fixed point of truth about God. To paraphrase T. S. Eliot, Jesus is "the still point of the turning world." And we are not. Relativism turns everyone into his or her own god, but Jesus will have none of that. Jesus claims to be the singular truth about God to whom we are all accountable. He is our ultimate source of authority.

What does this mean practically? Where do you seek the answers to life's basic questions? How do you define success? What is your life purpose? To whom do you look for ethical guidance? A disciple of Jesus submits their life to the authority, wisdom and guidance of Jesus. This is particularly true with regard to our core mission. We are to "go and make disciples of all nations" simply because Jesus has the authority to tell us what to do.

Jesus gives us his full backing. The second reason that Jesus declares his all-encompassing authority is that we go with his full backing. We have been given authorization by the God of the universe to carry out his mission. The image that comes to my mind is a scene from the old Western movies: the duly elected sheriff is in need of an impromptu posse to go after the bad guys so he rounds up all available men and slaps shiny badges on their chests as a symbol of their new authority. Jesus deputizes us to go make disciples, representing the unrivaled Ruler of the universe. As we go we have an inner security and continuing confidence that we have "the right man on our side."[5] As Paul affirms, "If God is for us, who can be against us?" (Romans 8:31).

HOW DO WE REPRESENT JESUS?

Yet as we have noted, we live in a relativist culture that can be an intimidating place for those of us who believe that Jesus is the universal Truth. Over the last few generations America has become increasingly secular (removal of the sacred from public life) and more religiously diverse (pluralistic). The public's view of Christians in some circles is that we are narrow-minded, judgmental and intolerant. The modern university can be an unfriendly environment to Christian students where the prevailing view toward religion is that it is at best outmoded and at worst part of the problem.

How might we respond to this culture of intimidation?

- Victimization: Portray ourselves as unfairly persecuted
- Arrogance: Act as if we have cornered the market on truth
- Humility: Grateful that God has found us

On the one hand we can come to see ourselves as *victims*. Victims feel sorry for themselves. "Woe is us. Look how badly we are being treated. Every other faith gets a pass, but it's the Christians who are being picked on. Feel sorry for us." Yet to do so is disempowering. We allow others to define us. Instead of coming across as a persecuted minority currying sympathy, we need simply to reclaim a deep assurance that we serve the One who has the last word about everything. How can we be victims when we have "the right man on our side"?

The opposite reaction to our culture of intimidation is to adopt an attitude of *arrogance*: we insulate ourselves as the ones who have cornered the market on truth. This can lead to a barricade mentality; not wanting to be tainted by the evils of this world, we isolate ourselves in our own Christian subculture by only associating with those with whom we feel safe. From inside the barricade of our own making we shout a message of smug moral judgment at a world gone astray. The result is that others are repelled, not attracted.

The way to navigate between the extremes of victimhood and arrogance is through the path of humility. Humility is born from a quiet and deeply rooted confidence that Jesus is who he claimed to be. D. T. Niles captures this spirit of humility when he described Christianity as "one beggar telling another beggar where to get food."[6] When we have a settled confidence in Jesus, we come across with the security that Michael Ramsay, the archbishop of Canterbury, displayed when was interviewed by Johnny Carson on *The Tonight Show*. Ramsay took his place on the couch next to the person Carson had just interviewed. No sooner had Ramsay sat down than he was accosted by the other guest. "You know what I don't like about your religion?" Looking a bit stunned, Ramsay asked, "What?" "I don't like your exclusiveness. You say Christ is the only way to God." The archbishop, without any defensiveness in his body language or voice, simply said, "Well, really. I never said that. Jesus was the one who made that claim. As a Christian I work with the documents of faith handed down in the church. I'm not really free to disagree or reinterpret Jesus. I am committed as a follower to teach what he taught."[7]

Jesus declares himself to be the unrivaled Ruler of the universe with the expectation that all who claim to be his followers would submit to him as the Lord of their lives. Then with his full backing his sends us to carry out his enterprise. There is never a need to be intimidated by rival human authorities nor to shield ourselves invulnerably by claiming a corner on the market of truth. When we represent Jesus we are pointing to the truth: he is the One whose authority flows out of his being.

Reading Study Guide

1. Think of someone in your life who occupied a place of elevated authority (coach, teacher, parent, military figure, pastor, etc.). What qualities did that person possess that gave him or her authority in your life?

2. What was it about Jesus that left the crowds "amazed"?

3. Does the overview of Jesus' divine prerogatives convince you that he was God? Why or why not?

4. What was it that convinced Bono that Jesus was God incarnate? Is this convincing to you? Why or why not?

5. How does the cultural spirit of relativism challenge Jesus' claim to ultimate authority? How do you experience the impact of cultural relativism in your life?

6. How can we convey a confidence in the truth about Jesus without coming across as either a victim of persecution or with an attitude of superiority? What can we learn from Archbishop Ramsay's model?

7. What would be the implications if you submitted your life to Jesus as the ultimate authority? Name one or two aspects that would be immediately affected.

---

[1]Quote from Abraham Kuyper's (then Prime Minister of the Netherlands) inaugural address at the dedication of the Free University of Amsterdam.

[2]Sydney J. Harris, "Authentic Teachers," *Phi Delta Kappan*, April 1964.

[3]Lee Stobel, *The Case for Faith* (Grand Rapids: Zondervan, 2000), 17.

[4]As quoted by Carolyn Weber in *Surprised by Oxford* (Nashville, TN: Thomas Nelson, 2011), 95-96.

[5]Martin Luther, *A Mighty Fortress Is Our God*, stanza 2.

[6]D. T. Niles, *That They May Have Life* (New York: Harper, 1951), 96.

[7]Robert E. Webber, *Ancient-Future Faith* (Grand Rapids: Baker Books, 1999), 190.

2 / Become Disciples

What's the Difference Between Disciples and Christians?

Looking Ahead

CORE TRUTH VERSE: "Therefore go and make disciples of all nations." (Matthew 8:19)
BIBLE STUDY: Mark 8:31-35
READING: Can You Be a Christian Without Being a Disciple?

 Core Truth

When Jesus commands us to "make disciples," what exactly does he mean?

We have adopted an unbiblical and costly distinction that says you can be a Christian without being a disciple. As commonly understood, a Christian is someone who has trusted Christ for forgiveness of sin and been assured of life forever with Jesus. The focus is on the benefits we receive from Jesus, not relinquishing our life to follow Jesus. Although our current definition of a Christian does not contain a need to actually follow Jesus, a disciple is someone who is following Jesus in order to learn how to be more like him.

• What key thoughts from the Core Truth stand out to you and why?

• What questions or issues does the Core Truth raise for you?

Inductive Bible Study Guide

In this session we continue to examine the Scripture text from session 1 that focused on the question, "Who do you say that I am?" Upon hearing Peter declare, "You are the Christ, the Son of the living God," Jesus reframes what it means to be the Messiah and lays the foundation for what he expects of those who will follow him. *Read Mark 8:31-35.*

1. In verse 31, Jesus paints a picture of how the Messiah will carry out his mission. What does Jesus' future hold?

2. Peter instantly goes from hero to goat. Why do you suppose Jesus was so stern with Peter in verse 33?

3. Note who Jesus is addressing in verse 33. Why is this significant?

4. Jesus outlines three requirements for anyone who wants to be his disciple:

   a. **Deny yourself:** In the context of our self-fulfillment/self-actualizing/be-all-that-you-can-be culture, the word *deny* sounds strange to our ears. What does it mean to deny yourself?

b. **Take up your cross:** If you lived in Jesus' day and saw someone carrying a cross behind a Roman soldier, what would you think was this person's future?

What might taking up a cross represent for a disciple?

c. **Follow me:** Why does "follow me" come after the two previous requirements?

5. According to verse 35, what is the payoff for those who take Jesus up on his offer?

⟨⟩ Reading: Can You Be a Christian Without Being a Disciple?

Dallas Willard shares a story from a pastor who challenged his congregation to become disciples. In response to this challenge, a woman said to her pastor after worship,

> I just want to be a Christian. I don't want to be a disciple. I like my life the way it is. I believe that Jesus died for my sins, and I will be with him when I die. Why do I have to be a disciple?[1]

How did we end up with this unfortunate yet quite common distinction that you can be a Christian without being a disciple?

Presently, the good news is largely framed in terms of receiving the benefits that Christ has purchased on the cross. This popular gospel is what I have come to call the *transactional gospel*. I call it a transaction because we see the message of salvation in accounting terms: our sin is entered as an eternal debit on our account; Jesus' death on the cross is our full payment for our sin; by faith his credit is transferred to our account, which cancels our debt and we are handed a receipt stamped "Paid in Full." Forgiveness of our sin debt and the assurance of eternal life is the gospel. Period.

In his book *The King Jesus Gospel* Scot McKnight argues that we have come to equate the gospel with "the plan of salvation" that is usually summarized in four points:[2]

- God loves you
- You messed up
- Jesus died for you
- Accept Jesus into your heart

The deal is sealed with the decision to receive Jesus Christ and trust him alone for forgiveness of sins and eternal life, followed by what we commonly call the sinner's prayer.

Right now, many of you may be saying to yourself, "So? What's your point? Isn't this the gospel?" In fact, this message has been so often repeated as the gospel that any challenge to it may seem like heresy.

If this isn't an accurate summary of the gospel, then we might ask, what was the gospel that Jesus proclaimed that led to people actually becoming disciples?

JESUS' GOSPEL

The book of Mark gives us the most succinct summary of Jesus' message: "After John was put in prison, Jesus went into Galilee, proclaiming the good news of God. 'The time has come,' he said. 'The kingdom of God has come near. Repent and believe the good news'" (Mark 1:14-15).

Interestingly enough, Jesus' proclamation of good news also had four points:

- The time has come
- The kingdom of God has come near
- Repent
- Believe the good news

Each phrase is packed with substance, so let's take a closer look.

The time has come. In his paraphrase *The Message*, Eugene Peterson captures Mark 1:15 simply as "Time's up!" This phrase conjures up the image of a pregnant woman who is closing in on the end of the nine-month waiting period. The culmination commences with birth pangs. Finally, they are five minutes apart. She announces to her husband, "It's time! Call the doctor! Let's go." The hour has arrived; the waiting is over.

So when Jesus says, "The time has come," he ties the gospel story back to the entire story of Israel and views himself as its completion.

The Greek word Jesus chooses for time is *kairos* as opposed to *chronos*. When we say, "What time is it?" we are using *chronos*. This is tick-tock time. One moment is the same as the next. In contrast *kairos* is opportunity time, a defining moment whose importance is not to be missed. *Kairos* says that everything will be different from this day forward.

The kingdom of God has come near. Jesus comes on the scene announcing the theme of his ministry as the proclamation of the "kingdom of God" and spends his last moments on earth following his death and resurrection speaking "about the kingdom of God" (Acts 1:3). In between there are 122 references to the kingdom of God or heaven with over ninety of these on the lips of Jesus. In order to understand Jesus' message of good news, we need to understand what he referred to as "the kingdom of God."

When Jesus came announcing the near presence of the kingdom of God, this would have stirred up images popular in Jesus' day. The Jewish people had longed for their promised Deliverer or Messiah (Christos) who would usher in the kingdom of God. One of the things that marked the difference between the Chosen People and all others was their view of history. The Jewish people actually believed history was going somewhere; it had a destination, as opposed to the meaningless repetitious cycles (summer, fall, winter, spring, endlessly; birth, life, death, rebirth, endlessly) of pagan cultures. The people of Israel believed in a Sovereign God who divided time into two major eras: *this age* followed by *the age to come*. (1) This age was torn asunder by sin and all its consequences, one of which was a shameful dominance by a foreign oppressor (at that time Rome). (2) But all of this would be supplanted by the inbreaking of the age to come (the kingdom of God).

A Messiah king would appear dramatically and establish a glorious age of the eternal reign of God on earth. All sin would be forgiven and expunged. The lion would lie down with the lamb. Swords would be beaten into plowshares. Best of all, the enemies of Israel would be vanquished, and the glory days of King David would be restored forever.

When Jesus came proclaiming, "The kingdom of God is at hand," you can imagine the surge of hope that pulsated through the veins of the people. Jesus the king was bringing the kingdom.

But Jesus was bringing in a very different kind of kingdom than was anticipated. From the beginning Jesus set about to indicate that their popular conception of a military leader was not what Jesus was going to be. Even by saying "the kingdom of God is at hand" was a way to be deliciously ambiguous about the nature of this kingdom. "At hand" can simultaneously mean "has arrived or is near" and "has come or is still to come." Which is it?

Both.

We live at a time between the times. This is why theologians have spoken of the kingdom of God as the "already but not yet." Jesus brings with him a kingdom that is very different than the one anticipated. How strangely this king wields his power. The kingdoms of men have symbols of power such as palaces and armies, yet King Jesus has nowhere to lay his head. Human kings rule over their realm on thrones, while King Jesus is lifted up on a cross.

In other words, the kingdom of God that Jesus brings on earth is a secret government that transcends geographic and political boundaries. It is truly a kingdom without borders. The interior structure of life in this kingdom is one dominated by the rule of grace and love. Our King calls us out of the world dominated by strife, tribalism and self-exaltation. Those who follow Jesus must change kingdoms. The apostle Paul wrote that the Father "has rescued us from the dominion of darkness and brought us into the kingdom of the Son he loves" (Colossians 1:13). It is only then that we step into the realm where we experience the benefits of the kingdom. However, to partake of the benefits you must realign your loyalties.

Repent. What is the entry way into the kingdom of God? Jesus is saying, "Here comes the kingdom of God, repent and believe the good news." King Jesus stands in our path and says, "You have a choice to make."

Repentance is Jesus' exclamation point, as if Jesus is saying, "Time's up! Wake up! Quit sleepwalking through life!" *Repent* is a jarring word and is meant to be so.

Repentance literally means, "Rethink your thinking!" The way you are thinking is leading you in the wrong direction because the kingdom of darkness in which you are currently dwelling has shaped your thinking. But the kingdom of God is based upon an entirely different set of values. Jesus says, "My kingdom will turn you right side up in an upside-down world."

To repent then is to begin to lay aside ways of thinking, habits, patterns, goals, ambitions, etc., that are based on a worldly set of assumptions. Jesus' ministry on earth demonstrated the contours of life in his kingdom. For example, James and John approached Jesus on the sly with a request to sit on his right and left hand when he came into his kingdom. What was their notion of the kingdom that Jesus would establish? It was based upon the view that the Messiah would usher in heaven on earth. Their view of self-importance and personal value meant that they wanted to be as close to the center of power as possible. But Jesus proceeds to flip their view of power on its head: "You know that those who are regarded as rulers of the Gentiles lord it over them, and their high officials exercise authority over them. Not so with you" (Mark 10:42-43). What Jesus was saying to James and John is that they had been captured by the world's view of power and value, not his.

If we want to be great in Jesus' kingdom, kneeling before others is the appropriate posture. The King never expects of his followers what he has not already modeled, giving "his life as a ransom for many" (Mark 10:45).

When we enter Jesus' kingdom we are called to a new order of life. We begin to recognize through confession of sin that we have been heading entirely in the wrong direction. To repent means to make a U-turn.

Believe the good news. Certainly the good news is that we have wondrous new standing with God through Christ now that we have been made right. Our sin, which separates us from a holy God, has been forgiven, and our forever future is secure. Yet in our simplistic plan of salvation approach we have tended to trivialize the gospel into an easy "believism."

In the tradition in which he grew up, John Ortberg says that people often asked each other, "Have you trusted Christ?" which was code language for, "Have you prayed the prayer? Do you believe in an arrangement that has been made for you to get you into heaven when you die?"[3] But Jesus means far more than praying a formulaic prayer or assenting to a set of core beliefs, such as a creed. To believe the good news is active. Jesus invites us to live consistent with the good news and enter the kingdom of God. Put your trust in, lean into and place your weight upon King Jesus.

CONCLUSION

Can you be a Christian without being a disciple? Or to put it another way, can we just "use" Jesus to get into heaven when we die and not live for him during our earthly days? That whole concept is foreign to the New Testament. For Jesus, Paul or Peter, there was not a sliver of daylight between being a Christian and being a disciple, and there is no middle ground.

Reading Study Guide

1. The woman in the opening story distinguishes between being a Christian and a disciple. What might she say is the difference between the two?

2. Summarize what the author refers to as the "transactional gospel."

3. What are the differences between the transactional gospel and Jesus' gospel?

4. How should Jesus' gospel of the kingdom of God shape our understanding of what it means to be a disciple? How does Jesus' gospel lead directly to becoming a disciple, as opposed to simply being a Christian as the woman in Dallas Willard's story understood it?

5. The means of entry into the kingdom of God is through repentance. What are you doing when you repent?

6. How has this teaching changed your understanding of the gospel and therefore what it means to be a disciple?

---

[1]Dallas Willard, *Renovation of the Heart* (Colorado Springs, CO: NavPress, 2002), 245.
[2]Scot McKnight, *The King Jesus Gospel* (Grand Rapids: Zondervan, 2011), 73.
[3]John Ortberg, "Are You Making Better Christians or More Disciples?" Willow Creek Community Church Reveal Conference 2008, Willow Creek Association Resources.

3 / Go

Reach All People

CORE TRUTH VERSE: "Therefore go and make disciples of all nations." (Matthew 28:19)
BIBLE STUDY: Luke 24:36-48; Acts 1:1-8
READING: Be Contagious and Share the Good Infection

⟳ Core Truth

What is the compelling spirit that flows through a disciple of Jesus?

A disciple instinctively moves toward those in need of the good news of Christ's redeeming love. This "go-spirit," the first characteristic of a disciple, expresses itself in at least three ways: (1) A disciple plays a role in the mission to spread the fame of Jesus to "every nation, tribe, people and language" (Revelation 7:9). (2) A disciple is a relational link to the good news of Jesus. (3) A disciple demonstrates the good news of Jesus through deeds of compassion and justice.

• What key thoughts from the Core Truth stand out to you and why?

• What questions or issues does the Core Truth raise for you?

Inductive Bible Study

In this study we will interlace the closing portion of Luke's gospel with his introduction to the book of Acts. They reinforce and amplify each other. In doing so we catch the drama of Jesus' post-resurrection appearances as well his instructions for the apostles to go as his witnesses. *Read Luke 24:36-47 and Acts 1:1-3, 8.*

1. In Luke 24:36-43 and Acts 1:1-3, how does Jesus reassure the eleven that they should believe what their eyes were seeing?

2. What role do these convincing proofs play in their call to be witnesses?

3. What attitude and emotion is Luke trying to capture when he writes that the disciples "still did not believe it because of joy and amazement"? (Luke 24:41)

4. According to Luke 24:44, how does Jesus tie his life and mission into the broader story of God's work through the people of Israel (see also Luke 24:27)? Why is this important?

5. Summarize in your own words the core message that Jesus revealed from his guided tour of the Law of Moses, the Prophets
   and the Psalms in Luke 24:45-47.

6. The disciples were called to be witnesses of all that they had seen
   (Luke 24:48; Acts 1:8). How are we called to be witnesses today?

7. What do you find challenging about being a witness for Christ
   with your

   - family?

   - friends?

   - neighbors?

   - work associates?

   - acquaintances?

⏴⏵ Reading: Be Contagious and Share the Good Infection

"If you build it, he will come." This was the whispered message that the novice Iowa farmer Ray Kinsella heard emanating from his cornfields in the 1989 fantasy film *Field of Dreams*. The meaning: Ray, if you turn some of your cornfields into a baseball diamond, Shoeless Joe Jackson and the seven other banned players from the 1919 Chicago White Sox will materialize. People will come from far and wide to watch the magic on the field.

There is a version of this fantasy that is still alive in the church today. The belief is if we do church with excellence, we will not be able to keep people away. If there is engaging preaching, great music, a high-energy youth program, first class facilities, etc., then people will flock to us. The assumption is that the unbelieving world is only waiting for quality programming. "If you build it, *they* will come."

Yet even in the best of times when the church played a more central and respected role in society, the if-you-build-it-they-will-come mentality should never define our strategy. Instead of saying, "Let people come to you," Jesus said, "Go!" Move out. Never keep the good news to yourself. As C. S. Lewis states, we have caught the "good infection." We need to be contagious.[1]

In our last session we saw that Jesus' presence was to be equated with the kingdom of God. Though his original audience may have heard this initially in geographical terms (the return of Israel's glory days), Jesus had a far wider scope in mind. To borrow a modern image, Jesus came to establish a kingdom without borders.

Jesus' kingdom does not recognize the boundaries on the map we call nation-states. His kingdom supersedes these manmade, sometimes changing designations in order to create an international community with King Jesus as it recognized ruler.

When Jesus tells us to *get up* and *go*, he is inviting disciples to

- join the mission to spread the fame of Jesus to "the ends of the earth";
- be a relational link to the good news of Jesus; and
- live out his "go agenda" through acts of compassion and justice.

JOIN THE MISSION

Our Lord is forming a people that cut across all the boundaries of language, culture, economics, race, etc. Yet the wonder of it all is that regardless of our widely varied backgrounds, the same Holy Spirit infects all believers. I have a vivid memory of when this truth first deeply penetrated my awareness. My wife, our ten-year-old daughter and I were waiting by the baggage carousel in Amsterdam's Schiphol Airport. I was there to attend the 1986 Billy Graham International Conference for Itinerant Evangelists. Suddenly, the terminal was transformed with the most glorious music. Every head turned in the direction of approximately fifty African men rhythmically dancing and singing praise to Jesus in two side-by-side rows as they seemed to float in our direction. Immediately the Holy Spirit in me connected with the same Spirit that indwelled these brothers. Our life circumstances could not have been more different, yet we were one. This snapshot is what Jesus intended from the beginning.

Andrew Walls, a recognized expert in the changing face of world Christianity, observes that of the major world religions only Christianity has continually shifted its geographical center. The other major world religions have not strayed far from where they began: Islam emanates from Mecca, its city of origin; Buddhism has not strayed far from its roots in the Far East (i.e., Tibet and China); and Hinduism is integral to the national identity of India and Nepal. In contrast, Christianity has shown an amazing capacity to adapt to every culture and shift its center without changing its core message.

To dramatize this shifting center, consider the breathtaking transformation of the state of world Christianity since 1900. In 1900 Christianity was largely considered a Western religion with a European imprint. Today we can now say that the face of Christianity is largely Asian, Latin American and African. In 1900 there were essentially no Christian churches in South Korea. Today in Seoul, the nation's capital, there are 7,500 Christian churches. In addition, 29 percent of the South Korean population is Christian. In 1949 when Mao Zedong came to power in China the combined population of Roman Catholic and Protestant believers was about one million. Today we know that there are more professing followers of Jesus in China than there are official members of the communist party.[2] Yet nothing compares to the runaway growth of Christ followers in Africa. In 1900 approximately 9 percent of sub-Saharan Africa was Christian whereas by 2010 that number had jumped to 63 percent. When we combine African and Latin American Christianity, by 2050 only 1 in 6 Christians will be white and the Global South will be its new center.

Jesus commanded us to "make disciples of all *ethnē.*" To translate *ethnē* as nation-state is misleading. If the Great Commission could be accomplished by simply planting a church in every recognized nation-state (e.g., United States, Russia, etc.), then the job would be done. But if we think of *ethnē* in terms of people groups, each with their own distinct language and culture, then there is a great task still before us.

What is the task that remains? The Joshua Project's latest census is that there are 16,619 distinct people groups that spill across national borders.[3] Of this, there are still some 6,971 "unreached people groups"—any group that does not have a vital enough Christian church in their language and culture so that they can hear the message in their native tongue—that account for 42 percent of the world's population or approximately 3 billion people. A vast majority of these unreached people exist within what has been dubbed the 10/40 window.[4] We can actually quantify the task before us—what a great time to be alive!

BEING A RELATIONAL LINK TO THE GOSPEL

Let's bring this "go" focus even closer to home. Jesus said, "You will receive power when the Holy Spirit comes on you; and you will be my witnesses in Jerusalem, and in all Judea and Samaria, and to the ends of the earth" (Acts 1:8).

Picture concentric circles of outward movement. The inner circle is made up of "Jerusalem and Judea." This was home territory for the apostles. The equivalent for us are the people within our circle of influence: family, friends, neighbors and work associates. The second concentric circle is "Samaria." The Samaritans were those the apostles had been taught to shun. For us these are the people we avoid because they are different from us. Finally, the third concentric circle is "the ends of the earth." This echoes the prophet Isaiah who said, "I will also make you a light for the Gentiles, that my salvation may reach to the ends of the earth" (Isaiah 49:6).

We have a story to tell about what Christ has done in our own life. A witness is someone who simply and accurately tells about what they have seen and heard. Our witness is to tell what difference the grace of Christ has made in our life. We have something to offer because we have a treasure that we cannot keep to ourselves. The apostle Paul said that the more he was aware of Christ's grace, the more he worked to make sure others knew about it (1 Corinthians 15:9-11). When Paul was forced to defend his faith, he simply told the story of his conversion (see Acts 9; 22; 26).

For most of us, our witness will be to those in our same language and culture (Jerusalem and Judea) or perhaps one language or cultural step removed (Samaria), such as international students in our midst. In New Testament times the good news spread largely through family networks called *oikos* or households. Family, friends, work associates, neighbors, etc., serve as our primary sphere of influence as well.

We are motivated to share our faith—to be contagious Christians—because we cannot imagine the people we love perishing without the opportunity to know the One who gave his life for them. If it is through us that people can hear about God revealing himself in Jesus, that Jesus bridged the gap between ourselves and a Holy God, and that the mystery of the identity of God has been made known, then how can we keep this to ourselves? It is the reception of this message that removes people from under the eternal wrath of God and places them under the sunlight of his love.

By living as winsome followers of Jesus, we can help people overcome negative stereotypes that many may have of Christians. Sheldon Vanauken and his wife, Davy, came to Oxford University as students in the early 1950s with the attitude that Christians "were necessarily stuffy, hide-bound, or stupid—people to keep one's distance from." Vanauken continues:

> Yet the first people we seemed to fall in with at Oxford were keen, deeply committed Christians. We liked them so much that we forgave them for it. We began, hardly knowing we were doing it, to revise our opinions, not of Christianity but of Christians. . . . The sheer quality of the Christians we met at Oxford shattered our stereotype. . . . The astonishing fact sank home: our own contemporaries could be at once highly intelligent, civilized, fun to be with—and Christian.[5]

This may be the first step some need to even consider who Jesus is to them.

There is an apocryphal story that imagines a conversation between the archangel Gabriel after Jesus ascended back to the Father.

Gabriel asks Jesus, "Well, how did it go? Did you complete your mission to save the world?"

Jesus replies, "Well, yes and no. I modeled a godly life for about thirty years. I preached to a few thousand Jews in one corner of the Roman Empire. I died for the sins of the world and promised that those who believe in me will live forever. And I burst forth from the tomb on the third day to show my circle of 120 frightened followers that my life and story are God's way to save the world. Then I gave the Holy Spirit to those 120 and left them to finish the task."

"You mean," Gabriel asked in amazement, "your whole plan to save the world depends on that ragtag bunch of fishermen, ex-prostitutes and tax collectors?"

"That's right," Jesus replied.

"But what if they fail?" Gabriel persists with growing alarm. "What's your back-up plan?"

"There is no back-up plan. I am counting on them," Jesus said confidently.[6]

We are the plan.

ACTS OF COMPASSION AND JUSTICE

One of the ways to reshape people's impression of Christ and his followers is to see the message undergirded with acts of service. Jesus said as much, "Let your light shine before others, that they may see your good deeds and glorify your Father in heaven" (Matthew

5:16). Peter echoes Jesus words, "Live such good lives among the pagans that . . . they may see your good deeds and glorify God on the day he visits us" (1 Peter 2:12).

In one of his *New York Times* editorials, Nicholas Kristoff confirmed that it was only compassionate actions that opened him to the ministry of evangelicals. Even though he "disagrees strongly with most evangelical Christians, theologically and politically," he wrote an editorial titled "God on Their Side." Kristoff recounts the story of seventeen-year-old Sonia Angeline and her rescue from the town garbage dump in Mozambique: after four days of labor pains, she was a hairsbreadth from death. She didn't have the money to take a taxi to the hospital until Katrin Blackert, a twenty-three-year-old volunteer with Iris Ministries, encountered her on her regular visits to children in the dump. Blackert paid for the cab and saved Sonia's life. After observing this kind of ministry, Kristoff was forced to conclude, "But I'm convinced that we should celebrate the big evangelical push into Africa because the bottom line is that it will mean more orphanages, more schools, and above all, more clinics and hospitals." [7]

Pastor Robert Lewis issued this challenge: "Unless the church rediscovers its primary role as bridge builder, the incarnational power of the gospel will remain hidden, and the credibility to reach a culture of cynical, experiential, and spiritually hungry souls will be lost. . . . People will simply no longer listen to or attend churches that seem incapable of living out what is preached. Bridges of influence—tangible and evident through the lifestyles and good works of believers—are the only answer."[8]

In order to be "go" disciples we need to build loving relationships to those near us, share the good news and confirm words with good deeds.

Reading Study Guide

1. What is the difference between a "come" vs. "go" mentality?

2. Share a cross-cultural experience, if you have one, where you sensed "the spirit of Jesus" in a person or people quite different from yourself.

3. In Acts 1:8, Luke describes the widening circles of gospel progression. What do each of these locations represent to the original hearers and now to you?

   • Jerusalem and Judea:

   • Samaria:

   • Ends of the earth:

4. What stereotypes do people have of Christians?

5. How could your lifestyle shatter these false images?

6. What is your story of God's grace that you could share with others?

7. Why are acts of service so vital for confirming the message of the gospel?

8. Where might the Lord be calling you to serve the world as his instrument of compassion and justice?

---

[1]C. S. Lewis, *Mere Christianity* (New York: MacMillan, 1952), 149.

[2]It is very difficult to get a definitive number on the followers of Christ in China. Estimates range widely from 69 million to 150 million, fully 10 percent of the population. World Christian Database, Center for the Study of Global Christianity at Gordon-Conwell Theological Seminary, www.worldchristiandatabase.org.

[3]Joshua Project, "Global Statistics," joshuaproject.net/global_statistics.

[4]Joshua Project, "What is the 10/40 Window?," joshuaproject.net/resources/articles /10_40_window.

[5]Sheldon Vanauken, *A Severe Mercy* (San Francisco, CA: Harper & Row, 1977), 77.

[6]Ronald J. Sider, *Living Like Jesus: Eleven Essentials to Growing a Genuine Faith* (Grand Rapids: Baker, 1996), 11.

[7]Nicholas Kristoff, "God on Their Side," *New York Times*, September 27, 2003.

[8]Robert Lewis, *The Church of Irresistible Influence* (Grand Rapids: Zondervan, 2001), 177.

4 / Baptize

Enter the Circle Dance of Love

LOOKING AHEAD

CORE TRUTH VERSE: "Baptizing them in the name of the Father and of the Son and of the Holy Spirit." (Matthew 28:19)
BIBLE STUDY: John 17:1-5, 20-26
READING: Welcome to the Circle Dance of Love

⮂ Core Truth

Why does Jesus include baptism as the second characteristic for what it means to be a disciple?

Within the Christian community baptism has acquired broad significance: (1) a public declaration of faith; (2) a sign of inclusion in the church; (3) cleansing from the guilt of sin and a fresh start and (4) identification with the death and resurrection of Jesus (Romans 6:3-4). Though these associations with baptism are all true and deeply meaningful, they do not sufficiently capture why Jesus included baptism as a critical element in his definition of a disciple. In addition, through baptism Jesus is affirming that a disciple is one who is welcomed into the eternal circle of the loving God who is Father, Son and Holy Spirit.

- What key thoughts from the Core Truth stand out to you and why?

- What questions or issues does the Core Truth raise for you?

Inductive Bible Study

At the close of the section of Scripture known as the Upper Room Discourse (John 13–17), we are allowed to eavesdrop on Jesus' final extended conversation with his Father just prior to the cross. Listen in to this most poignant and tender dialogue as Jesus pours out his heart to his Father. *Read John 17:1-5, 20-26.*

1. What is Jesus' definition of eternal life? (vv. 2-3)

2. What does this tell us about the relationship between Jesus and the Father?

3. Jesus prays for the unity of his followers (vv. 20-23). What is the purpose of our unity?

4. How does Jesus describe the interrelationship between believers, the Father and himself?

5. What is it that Jesus longs for his followers to experience? (vv. 24-26)

6. Jesus has given us two windows into his self-awareness that he existed in a loving relationship with his Father "before the world began" (v. 5) and "before the creation of the world" (v. 24). What does this indicate about the nature of life within the Trinity for all eternity?

7. How does Jesus' inclusion of you in his relationship with the Father impact your understanding of your value to God?

 ## Reading: Welcome to the Circle Dance of Love

In the seventh century John of Damascus, a Greek theologian, described the relationships within the Trinity as *perichoresis*, or a "circle dance." *Choros* is a festive dance performed on occasions such as weddings or banquets. Adding *peri* as a prefix, meaning "round about," emphasizes the circularity of the dance. John pictured the one God who is three persons in a dance of intimacy, equality and unity, always deferring in love and honor to one another. This is the God who dances at the center of the universe and invites us to join in.

Because it took me a long time to grasp the nature of life within the Trinity, the meaning of "baptizing them in the name of the

Father and of the Son and of the Holy Spirit" eluded me. Why had Jesus included this second characteristic of a disciple at the heart of his definition? There was this continual, nagging thought: "Why is baptism so central to what it means to be a disciple?" Or as one person sarcastically quipped: "What does getting wet have to do with it?" What is the depth of significance here?

Then it finally dawned on me that I had misplaced the emphasis. I was simply focused on the word "baptizing," viewing what followed as the accompanying formula. For years as a pastor, I used the usual script: "I baptize you in the name of the Father and of the Son and of the Holy Spirit." I thought Jesus was simply writing lines for a book of worship. But what I have come to see is that baptism is the means through which we enter into the dance of the eternal three-person community.

From the moment humanity stepped out of the dance and lost the harmony and fellowship with God in the Garden of Eden, God has set about to restore what has been lost. Because of the redemptive work of Jesus Christ, baptism into the name of the triune God signifies that the work of restoration has been completed.

Let's see if I can catch the depth of meaning here through this paraphrase: "As you are *going*, make disciples of all nations, *immersing them into the life of the eternal community of love who coexists as the Father and the Son and the Holy Spirit.*" Baptism literally is immersion: *into* is the more accurate rending rather than *in* because it implies a fusion of our life with God's life. And as we shall see, the three-person God is the original loving community.

We get our first glimpse of God's revelation as a three-person being in the creation account in Genesis 1 where we are given the answer to the age-old question, "Why did God create human beings in the first place?"

Genesis 1 begins with the well-known phrase, "In the beginning God created the heavens and the earth." For the next twenty-five verses the six days of creation unfold with a repeated formula: "God said, let there be . . ." But then in the latter part of the sixth day there is a dramatic shift in the pattern, as if God had been warming up for the big event. There is movement from the impersonal, "Let there be . . . and it was so," to the personal, "Let us make mankind in our image, in our likeness" (Genesis 1:26). The direction toward which all creation was headed, the crown jewel, is the appearance of human beings who reflect the image of the One who made us. The difference between all the rest of creation and human beings is that people alone reflect the personal image and likeness of their Creator.

Yet exactly what is this image of God that humans reflect? It is found in the very unusual way that God chooses to speak of himself. There is one God, yet he says, "Let *us* make mankind in *our* image, in *our* likeness" (Genesis 1:26, emphasis mine). Why does God speak about himself in the plural?

Now that we live on this side of the incarnation of God's Son, Jesus Christ, and the presence the Holy Spirit who indwells the church, this mystery has been revealed. Through the greater light of the New Testament we can see that from all eternity God is one being who is three persons.

So what does this tell us about what it means for humans to be made in God's image? Prior to creation God existed as the first loving community, a being whose very essence is relationship. In other words, just as God's image is a relational one, so we are made for relationship with God and each other. Michael Lloyd writes, "It is relationships that matter most to us because we were made not only for relationship, but made by Relationship. We were made in the image of God—and God is relationship."[1]

Let's think about this. We affirm with the apostle John that the core characteristic of God is love (1 John 4:7-21). Yet if for all eternity God was simply a solitary being, how could he be a God of love? C. S. Lewis writes, "Love is something one person has for another. If God were a single person, then before the world was made, He was *not* love."[2] And Baxter Kruger adds, "From all eternity, God is not alone and solitary, but lives as Father, Son and Holy Spirit in rich and glorious fellowship of utter oneness. The Trinitarian life is a great dance of unchained communion and intimacy, fired by passionate, self-giving, other-centered love and mutual delight."[3]

If God were a solitary being before he created us, then the creation of humans would have fulfilled some deficit within him. Was God lonely and needed companionship? If God needed us to complete him it would make us simply a means to his end. But the apostle Paul reminds us of God's self-sufficiency when he addresses the Greeks in Athens: "The God who made the world and everything in it is the Lord of heaven and earth and does not live in temples built by human hands. And he is not served by human hands, as if he needed anything. Rather, he himself gives everyone life and breath and everything else" (Acts 17:24-25). Our God did not create to fill some void; He created out of the fullness of love. Meister Eckhart, fourteenth-century German mystic, wonderfully said that God created out of the "laughter of the Trinity."[4]

Let me see if I can bring this down to earth with a homespun story. My wife and I were married in 1969. It was during the height of the counter-cultural revolution that was going on in the midst of the Vietnam War, civil rights movement, etc. This was also the era of freedom to be able to be and do as one pleases. Children at that time were considered an impediment to this freedom, so for the first five years of our married life we held to our "no child policy."

Yet unbeknownst to each other, we both began to change our minds about wanting to have children, but it was one of those marriage issues that we were both afraid to raise. So when we suspected my wife was pregnant (all the usual signs), off to the doctor she went to confirm our suspicions. A few days later we got the call from the doctor's office saying that the tests had come back negative. "No, you are not pregnant." It was only then that we acknowledged to each other how disappointed we were with this news. What surprised us was that just the thought of having a child made us long for a child. We wanted a product of our together love on whom to bestow love. (Fortunately, the doctors were wrong; we do have a daughter to prove it.)

This story illustrates how the community of the triune God could not contain his love within himself. There was so much joy to be shared that humans were created out of the overflow of God's love in order to be folded into this love. To be made in the image of God is to be made for relationship—with God and with others.

But where do we get a glimpse into life within the Trinity? What is the nature of this life into which we are included?

THE FATHER-SON RELATIONSHIP

Thanks to Jesus, the relational life within the Trinity is no longer a complete mystery. Through the relationship between Jesus and the Father we get to see the dance of love that we are invited to join. It is Jesus who introduces us to his Father. Throughout the entirety of the Old Testament God is referred to as Father just fifteen times, and never addressed as such in prayer. In the Gospels, God is called Father 179 times, and over one hundred times in the gospel of John alone. When Jesus teaches us to pray, he tells us to address God as "Our Father."

To understand more fully what it means to be "immersed into the life of the three-person God," I want to open three windows for us to look into the relationship Jesus shares with his Father.

Window No. 1: Jesus' Baptism (Mark 1:9-11). Our first window comes from the dramatic scene when Jesus is launched into public ministry as he presents himself to John for baptism. As Jesus comes out of the waters of baptism, we see the presence of the three-person

God. The Holy Spirit alights upon Jesus in the form of a dove, signifying the power available for his ministry (Mark 1:10). The Father speaks affirmation of his Son saying, "You are my Son, whom I love; with you I am well pleased" (Mark 1:11). I visualize the Father grasping the shoulders of his Son, looking deeply and intently in his eyes and saying, "As you head off into our ministry, I want you to know above all else how I feel about you: You are my beloved and I couldn't be prouder." Eugene Peterson offers this tender rephrasing that captures the pride of the Father, "You are my Son, chosen and marked by my love, pride of my life" (Mark 1:11 *The Message*).

Window No. 2: Jesus in the Garden of Gethsemane (Mark 14:32-36). A second window into the Son's life with the Father occurs in the Garden of Gethsemane. Just hours before his appointment with the cross, Jesus finds a lonely place to pour out his heart in anguish to his Father. It is here that Jesus addresses his Father in the most intimate of terms, "*Abba,* Father. . . . Take this cup from me [meaning death on the cross]. Yet not what I will, but what you will" (Mark 14:36). This was the moment for which Jesus came, but if there was ever a time when the Son would doubt the love of his Father, it was then. Jesus must have been recalling these words: "You are my Son, whom I love; with you I am well pleased." When Jesus was beset emotionally, with the abandonment of the cross before him, he turned to his Father.

Window No. 3: Jesus' Final Prayer (John 17:1-5, 20-26). A third window into the intimate connection between Father and Son comes when Jesus prepares to offer his final prayer for his disciples. There are moments in the Bible when what is conveyed is so personal that it feels as if we are intruding, yet here we gain a glimpse of the abiding affection between the Father and Son. Jesus says, "And now, Father, glorify me in your presence with the glory I had with you before the world began" (John 17:5). How do we even begin to capture the depth of what Jesus is feeling? The best way I can put it is that Jesus is homesick—missing face-to-face intimacy with his father, and longing for the familiar, the embrace and the exchange of love. He can't wait to get back to what he once had, prior to his taking on human flesh. Essentially Jesus is saying, "Bring me home, Father. I miss you."

Jesus then turns the focus of his prayer from his yearnings to his longings for us. He prays that his followers down through the ages would be woven into the fabric of union of the Father and Son. "I pray . . . that all of them may be one, Father, just as you are in me and I am in you. May they also be in us" (John 17:20-21). And he concludes this prayer with the most amazing statement. He says that the circle of Trinity has been opened and that this community of love has welcomed us in: "I have made you known to them, and will continue to make you known in order that the love you have for me may be in them and that I myself may be in them" (John 17:26).

Here is a human analogy in order that we might better understand the circle dance of love. Imagine that you were raised in a home where a shared family meal was a rarity. There were not consistent family patterns, so everyone was on their own. Frankly you didn't even know what you didn't have. As good fortune would have it, you became friends with someone who spoke respectfully and lovingly of their parents and had siblings they were not embarrassed to be around. One night your friend invites you to join the family for dinner. The atmosphere around the table is nothing like you have ever experienced. A beaming father tells you what a delight it is to have you to join them. A home-cooked meal is brought to the table with each family member taking their part in making sure the table was set. The conversation turns to the events of the day and each person takes interest in drawing out the others. Humor comes naturally in the form of needling each other with playfulness. There is lightness in the air. The family lingers around the table because they enjoy each other so much. You sit there thinking, *I didn't even know this kind of loving family was possible.* As the plates are being cleared, the mother says to you, "You are welcome to join us any time. Consider yourself a part of the family." As you ponder this experience, you think, *This is what I wanted all my life and I didn't even know it!*

The truth of the trinitarian embrace is that we are adopted into the family of God and obtain a similar position before the Father that Jesus has. The Father says to us, "You are my child, marked and chosen by my love, the pride of my life." We get to address the Father just as Jesus did, calling him our "Abba," because his Spirit now dwells in us. This is the way Paul captures our new identity: "The Spirit you received does not make you slaves, so that you live in fear again; rather, the Spirit you received brought about your adoption to sonship. And by him we cry, '*Abba,* Father.' The Spirit himself testifies with our spirit that we are God's children" (Romans 8:15-16).

To be made in the image of God is to be made for relationship. For all eternity God has been the first loving community and he made us to be included in this community of love. To know that we are the delight of the Father's heart and that we are taken into the circle dance of trinitarian love that will one day flow through us unimpeded is what it means to baptize "in the name of the Father and the Son and the Holy Spirit."

Reading Study Guide

1. What feelings are evoked when you picture the Trinity as a kind of circle dance?

2. Consider Jesus' second discipleship characteristic, *immersing them into the life of the eternal community of love who coexists as the Father and the Son and the Holy Spirit.* What does it mean to be immersed into this community?

3. What does it mean for humans to be created in God's image?

4. What are the implications if God were simply a solitary being from all eternity?

5. How does the analogy offered of deciding to have a child relate to how God regards us?

6. What do the three windows display to you about the nature of the Father-Son relationship?

7. How do these windows give you a glimpse into the life we are invited to share?

8. How has the personal invitation contained in "baptizing them into the name of the Father and of the Son and of the Holy Spirit" changed or shaped your understanding of God's relationship to you?

[1]Michael Lloyd, *Café Theology* (London, England: Alpha International, 2005), 294.
[2]C. S. Lewis, *Mere Christianity* (New York: Macmillan, 1952), 151.
[3]Baxter Kruger, *The Shack Revisited* (New York: Faith Words, 2012), 62.
[4]W. J. de Kock, *Out of My Mind: Following the Trajectory of God's Regenerative Story* (Eugene, OR: Wipf and Stock, 2014), 53.

5 / Teach

Fall in Line Behind Jesus

Looking Ahead

CORE TRUTH VERSE: "Teaching them to obey everything I have commanded you." (Matthew 28:20)
BIBLE STUDY: John 14:15, 23-24; 15:9-17
READING: A Long Obedience in the Same Direction

Core Truth

What is the ultimate sign of our love for Jesus?

Jesus states with unambiguous clarity that our love for him will be confirmed by obedience to his commands. But he does not say this like some power-crazed cult figure who demands mindless and robotic compliance. On the contrary, Jesus wins our submission to his authority through his demonstrative love as evidenced in the cross. Obedience, therefore, is inseparable from trust in our Lord's goodness. When we do all that Jesus commands we are also doing what is best for us. Disciples are those who have made it their intent to have the life of Jesus formed in them.

- What key thoughts from the Core Truth stand out to you and why?

- What questions or issues does the Core Truth raise for you?

Inductive Bible Study

Jesus gathered his disciples in the upper room where he gave them his final counsel before his divine appointment with the cross. Put yourself in the room with the disciples and listen carefully to these last words of a dying man. *Read John 14:15, 23-24; 15:9-17.*

1. Put into your own words why keeping his commands (obeying his teaching) is the demonstration of our love for Jesus. (vv. 14:23-24)

2. What is Jesus' promise, both positively and negatively, regarding keeping or obeying his commands/teaching?

3. What do you think Jesus means when he says, "We will come to them and make our home with them"?

4. What is the relationship between love and obedience? (vv. 15:9-17)

5. What is the greatest expression of love? (vv. 15:12-13)

6. Jesus says he no longer considers his disciples servants, but friends (v. 15:15). What is the difference between servant and friend?

7. How might being considered a friend of Jesus impact our motivation to keep his commands?

8. Let's personalize Jesus' call: "(Your name), I have placed my eye upon you, called you to myself, so that you would go and bear fruit." What does hearing your name connected to this call do in you?

🕶 Reading: A Long Obedience in the Same Direction

Without obedience to authority life would be chaos. Every day of our lives we count on people to obey the law. Every time we get behind the wheel of a car we have made a huge assumption that people will obey the rules of the road and stay within the painted lines. As we approach a stop sign or a red light, we assume that others have so internalized the meaning of the symbol that they too will halt. If we could not depend on this we would not dare leave our homes. Anarchy and destruction would ensue if individuals said to themselves, "There is nothing in that symbol that can actually cause me to stop.

I will just roll right on through." It is only as authority is honored that safety is ensured.

In this third characteristic of a disciple, we are told that followers of Jesus submit themselves to be taught "to obey everything I [Jesus] have commanded you." Throughout our reflections we have been stringing together concepts of order: Jesus' all-encompassing *authority* . . . the gospel of the *kingdom* of God . . . and now *obedience* to his commands. King Jesus has a new way of life intended for us, "For he has rescued us from the dominion of darkness and brought us into the kingdom of the Son he loves" (Colossians 1:13). There is an order of life in his kingdom that followers are to adopt.

In the space of just nine words ("teaching them to obey everything I have commanded you") Jesus has summarized our vocation, our calling, our life endeavor. We are to bring our lives in line with Jesus' explicit intentions.

Let's explore Jesus' meaning one phrase at a time.

TEACHING THEM

When we put together "make disciples" with "teaching them" we are talking about a lifelong endeavor. "To disciple means 'to make students,' 'bring to school,' 'to educate.' . . . Work with people over time in an educative process of teaching Jesus."[1] This is what Eugene Peterson calls "a long obedience in the same direction."[2]

This "long obedience" requires that a disciple adopt a *training mentality*. If we have attempted to accomplish anything of significance we know what a training mentality is. Any athlete who wants to perform at some level of excellence knows that the game is won or lost on the practice field. Financial security into our retirement years will require the discipline of monthly investments. Whatever our career choice, be it lawyer or plumber, radiation technician, painter, doctor or contractor, will require sustained commitment to study or apprenticeship to master our field.

The apostle Paul uses an athletic image to capture the way we need to approach our vocation of obedience:

> Do you not know that in a race all the runners run, but only one gets the prize? Run in such a way as to get the prize. Everyone who competes in the games goes into strict training. They do it to get a crown that will not last, but we do it to get a crown that will last forever. (1 Corinthians 9:24-25)

Note Paul's *how-much-more* argument here. Athletes are willing to go into "strict training" to get a reward that fades quickly and is soon forgotten; *how much more* should we who are looking forward to an eternal reward be willing "to leave it all on the field." Dallas Willard sums it up succinctly when he says, "Grace is opposed to earning, but not opposed to effort."[3]

The presence of a training mentality is evidenced by

- a teachable spirit—a hunger and thirst to know Jesus and submit to His word; and

- a spiritual growth plan—a disciplined set of practices that serve as our regimen for obedience.

Teachable spirit. When I was a twenty-something seminary student right out of college a highly regarded seminary professor modeled for me a teachable spirit. After a distinguished career as a pastor, he became a faculty mentor. One day my wife informed that this same revered professor was on the phone and wanted to talk to me. I didn't even think he knew I existed. He had read an article I wrote on Jesus' model of disciplemaking. He wanted my permission to reprint the article to be used in his class. In that moment, he said all that I needed to know about a teachable spirit. He thought that this rookie had something to teach him and his students, even though he had been in the pastoral trenches over a lifetime. He never stopped learning regardless the source nor was he afraid to expose a gap in his knowledge.

We are teachable when we hunger to know God's Word and conform our lives to it. The late Charles Colson, founder of Prison Fellowship, served a short prison sentence because of his involvement in the Watergate cover-up under President Nixon. When he was released from prison he wanted to close this chapter and move on, but the truth of Scripture would not let him go. Colson wrote, "What 'radicalized' me was not prison, but taking to heart the truths revealed in Scripture. For it was the Bible that confronted me with a new awareness of my sin and need for repentance; it was the Bible that caused me to hunger for righteousness and holiness; and it was the Bible that called me into fellowship with the suffering."[4]

These two men have challenged me to assess how teachable I am.

Spiritual growth plan. As important as a passion for God's Word and a pliable spirit are, we need the structure and discipline of a plan to sustain our growth. Many of us have financial plans, educational plans, career plans and health plans, but what about a spiritual growth plan? A spiritual growth plan is our training regimen. A plan harnesses our passion into practices. We populate our spiritual growth plan with what are called *spiritual disciplines*. Spiritual disciplines are exercises or practices that tether our heart to the triune God and his Word in order for us to be obedient to his commands.

What are some elements to be included in our spiritual growth plan? A training regimen can be made up of two types of regular exercises: private and community disciplines. On a private level we learn to feed ourselves through regular consumption of Bible reading, prayer and reflection on God's Word. On a community level we gain strength with others through public worship and compassionate acts of service. Most importantly, we need the regularity of meeting with others in small groups for the express purpose of helping one another grow to be obedient followers of Christ (see sessions 6 and 7). I would highly recommend adopting a discipleship training manual that covers the foundational territory of the Christian faith. Without a curriculum you don't have a map to traverse the territory that you need to cover.[5]

As John Ortberg reminds us, "Following Jesus simply means learning from him to arrange my life around activities that enable me to live in the fruit of the Spirit. . . . Spiritual disciplines are to life what practice is to a game."[6]

The training mentality cultivates a teachable spirit combined with a plan for spiritual growth. But all of this is to what end?

TO OBEY

When it comes to Jesus' command "to obey," this immediately raises the issue of motivation. The very idea of obedience can have a negative association. It can be laden with "shoulds" and "oughts." The apostle Paul reminds us that as we meet the *shoulds* of the law or the *oughts* someone commands, we automatically recoil with resistance. Paul writes, "I would not have known what sin was had it not been for the law" (Romans 7:7). Others may associate obedience with fear of punishment. We obey to avoid the consequences of disobedience.

But "no one can be a disciple of Jesus because you think you *should*, you actually have to *want* it."[7] So how do we get beyond thinking that we should be disciples to actually wanting to be disciples? What is it that stirs our longings, desires and yearnings to want to obey Jesus' commands? This takes us back to Jesus' gospel we explored in session 2. We enter the relationship with Jesus through the door of repentance. King David said that the heart that delighted God was a "broken spirit; a broken and contrite heart" (Psalm 51:17). David was forced to peer into the depths of his personal abyss after his adultery with Bathsheba and the cover-up murder of her husband, Uriah. Submission and surrender to the will of Jesus only comes when we are in touch with the consequences of our own self-destructive will.

Yet our broken heart is immediately massaged to health because of the outpouring of God's mercy and grace. David begins Psalm 51 with a plea that was answered, "Have mercy on me, O God, according to your unfailing love; according to your great compassion blot out my transgressions" (Psalm 51:1). The Lord rushes to a heart that expresses its need and utter dependence on him. The Great Physician then writes a health plan that we are to follow for a complete recovery. "Perfect obedience would be perfect happiness if only we had perfect confidence in the power we are obeying."[8] We submit to God's plan because our best is found in him.

Jesus does not bludgeon us into submission to his will by simply pulling rank. He woos in love so that we want to choose him over other options. When Jesus stood before the disciples declaring their disciplemaking mission, he still bore permanent scars on his hands and puncture wounds in his side. What greater love could they imagine? A God who loves like that can be entrusted to guide us into fullness of life itself. The apostle Paul lays out the argument for the "want to" of obedience. "If God is for us, who can be against us? He who did not spare his own Son, but gave him up for us all—how will he not also, along with him, graciously give us all things?" (Romans 8:31-32). The only appropriate response to such love is to obey.

Obedience to Jesus' command becomes our heart's desire when we see the vision that Jesus has for our life. In her book *Hope Has*

Its Reasons, Becky Pippert tells the story of getting lost in Jerusalem. She had gotten off at the wrong bus stop and found herself in an Orthodox Hasidic Jewish neighborhood. She was rescued by a Hasidic Jewish man named Moshe who was a part of an ultra-orthodox community. Becky said to Moshe, "We have something in common. We are both religious." Moshe asked Becky, "Are you Jewish?" Becky replied, "No, I am a follower of Jesus." Moshe exclaimed, "I have never talked with a religious Christian before." Wondering if he would ever get another opportunity, they secretly made their way to Becky's apartment at her invitation.

Once they settled in Moshe began to pepper Becky with questions. What he wanted to know was what happens to human nature as a result of being in relationship with God through Christ. Becky responded by saying that when we put our faith in Christ, he gives us his Spirit, who transforms us day by day and enables us to live as new people with new power. Then he asked a very insightful question, "What is the essence of this new nature?" She listed the fruit of the Spirit from Galatians 5:22-23.

With all the eagerness of one with a hungry heart Moshe said, "Wait, say those words again." Becky again recited them. "Say them again," he asked.

Then Moshe said with wonderment, "What beautiful, beautiful words. Love, joy, peace, patience, kindness, goodness, faithfulness, gentleness, and self-control. Imagine it! All of these qualities come into your heart as a result of being in relationship with God. Just think, to receive the very nature of God as a gift. No more beating down the evil inclinations with negatives but rather fighting evil with positives, with the very attributes of God himself! Ah, what a precious gift you have inherited, Becky. Do not take it lightly."[9]

How could we not want the delicious qualities of the fruit of the Spirit to permeate our life? As our "want to" is aligned with Jesus' desire for us, we are drawn into a lifelong process of growing in obedience. It never ends.

EVERYTHING

Obedience for Jesus is not a multiple choice exam. We are to obey *everything* he commands. But if we are honest, we will note how selective we are. We tend to lean toward our Lord's message of accepting grace but lean away from some of the hard implications of obedience. We want to be forgiven for our debts or trespasses, but when it comes to forgiving those who have hurt us, we may not be so understanding. We see Jesus taking on insults and humiliation on the cross, but do we follow Jesus' model when we are insulted, humiliated or betrayed? I love viewing myself as the returning prodigal to whom the Father runs to embrace, but I don't gravitate easily to the hard work of recognizing myself as the judgmental, morally superior older brother who shuns the love of the Father. Keith Philips warns of this "dip and skip" method: we love to dip into the promises but we skip the commands.[10]

Following Jesus in some ways makes our life more complicated than less. But Jesus promises that in losing our life for his sake we actually find it (Luke 9:24).

I HAVE COMMANDED

Finally, we note the source of this call to obedience. Jesus is the one who is commanding. The wisdom of the church down through the ages is that obedience precedes knowledge. Philip Yancey writes, "I do not get to know God, then do his will, I get to know God by doing his will."[11] This truth came home to me when I committed myself to prison ministry in recent years. Throughout my life, I had heard people give testimony of their ministry to those behind bars. My inner response was, "God bless you. I am sure glad there are those who have that call, but I can't imagine myself relating to those kinds of people in those dangerous circumstances." But because some of my discipleship materials were being used in prisons, I responded to an invitation to go into maximum-security prison. To my utter amazement, I found that the Lord had actually given me the facility to connect with the men and they in turn with me. The words that the Lord used to make prison ministry a part of my weekly activities were spoken right at the end of my first visit. One of the inmates said in the presence of about fifty others, "We are the forgotten people, don't forget us." That was a Holy Spirit stab in the heart. Never was there a better commentary on what Jesus meant when he said, "Whatever you did for one of the least of these brothers and sisters of mine, you did for me" (Matthew 25:40). I tell people now, "I go to prison to see Jesus." I had to obey before I could know the heart of God.

Reading Study Guide

1. What is a training mentality?

2. Why is a training mentality necessary if we are going to "obey everything that Jesus commanded"?

3. From reading the stories of the professor and Charles Colson, how would you describe a teachable spirit?

4. How do these stories challenge you?

5. What is a spiritual growth plan? Why is it necessary?

6. What are some of the elements that lead us to a "want to" attitude of obedience?

7. How does Moshe's response to the fruit of the Spirit capture the "want to" motivation for obedience?

8. Think about the story of prison ministry. Why does obedience precede and lead to deeper knowledge of God?

9. Who rules your life? That is, who or what is competing for ultimate authority over you?

[1]Frederick Dale Bruner, *The Churchbook, Matthew 13-28* (Dallas, TX: Word, 1990), 1096.

[2]Eugene Peterson, *A Long Obedience in the Same Direction* (Downers Grove, IL: InterVarsity Press, 2000).

[3]Dallas Willard, *The Great Omission* (San Francisco, CA: Harper & Row, 2006), 34.

[4]Charles Colson, *Loving God* (Grand Rapids: Zondervan, 1987), 40.

[5]Greg Ogden, *Discipleship Essentials: A Guide to Building Your Life in Christ* (Downers Grove, IL: InterVarsity Press, 2007). This is one model that attempts to cover a broad spectrum of the foundations upon which to build our life in Christ.

[6]John Ortberg, *The Life You've Always Wanted* (Grand Rapids: Zondervan, 1997), 49.

[7]John Ortberg from his message titled, "Are We Making Better Christians or More Disciples?" October, 2008, Reveal Conference at Willow Creek Community Church. DVD available through Willow Creek Association Resources.

[8]Hannah Smith as quoted by Catherine Marshall, *Something More: In Search of a Deeper Faith* (New York: McGraw-Hill, 1974), 94.

[9]Rebecca Manley Pippert, *Hope Has Its Reasons* (Downers Grove, IL: InterVarsity Press, 2001), 182-83.

[10]Keith Philips, *The Making of a Disciple* (Old Tappan, NJ: Fleming H. Revell Co., 1981), 44.

[11]Philip Yancey, *Reaching for the Invisible God* (Grand Rapids: Zondervan, 2000), 89.

6 / Make Disciples

Jesus' Relational Way

LOOKING AHEAD

CORE TRUTH VERSE: "He appointed twelve that they might be with him." (Mark 3:14)
BIBLE STUDY: John 17:6-19
READING: Relationship, Relationship, Relationship

⟳ Core Truth

What does Jesus' practice of focusing on a few teach us about how disciples are made?

Jesus spent a major portion of his time with his disciples because that was the only way to transfer his manner, message and mission into their lives. Following Jesus' model, "disciples are made through intentional relationships where we walk alongside one another, encouraging, equipping and challenging each other to grow toward maturity in Christ. This includes equipping the disciple to teach others as well."[1]

• What key thoughts from the Core Truth stand out to you and why?

• What questions or issues does the Core Truth raise for you?

Inductive Bible Study

Jesus' ministry touched thousands but he trained twelve. Jesus gave his life on the cross for untold billions, but those billions would only know him because he focused on a few. In Jesus' final prayer for his disciples we see that he staked his entire mission on them. *Read John 17:6-19.*

1. What privileged knowledge and relationship did the disciples have with Jesus and the Father?

2. For what role(s) has Jesus prepared his disciples?

3. As Jesus prays for his disciples, what are his concerns for them?

4. The word *world* is used throughout this prayer (vv. 6, 9, 11, 13-16, 18). How is Jesus using *world* in this context?

5. What danger does Jesus anticipate the disciples will face and how will they be protected?

6. Jesus prays that his followers would not be "of the world" (v. 14) while still remaining in the world. What do you understand this to mean?

7. Identify two areas of your life where you sense that you are called to be different from the world even as you remain in it. What challenges might these present?

8. As you encounter these areas where you are called to be different, in what ways might you need to be protected from the evil one?

Reading: Relationship, Relationship, Relationship

"We need to think of the Bible not only as a *message* book, but also as a *method* book."[2] This means that Scripture not only gives us the content of the good news (message) but it also shows us how (method) to embed and multiply in and through the lives of would-be disciples.

I was fortunate enough to have a living embodiment of this truth. During my sophomore year in college I received a phone call from the junior high pastor at our church: "Greg, how would you like to be a part of a team of college students ministering to junior high kids on Wednesday nights?" One hundred thirty students were bouncing off the church gymnasium walls. Don needed reinforcements. I had no idea at the time how throwing my lot into the lives of these preteens would change my trajectory for a lifetime. Don gave us Jesus' mission to share his love with these young lives on their turf. Coming out of the stands onto the playing field energized me in a way that sitting in a pew listening to sermons never could.

But there was a bonus. Don not only gave us a mission, but also himself. Don would call to get together for some one-on-one time. I have vivid recollections of sitting on the bench next to the tennis court after batting the ball around. Don would invariably pull out his Bible and share some things with me that he was applying to his life. What impressed me about Don was his transparency. He didn't sugarcoat the challenge of discipleship. He showed me Scriptures that exposed needed changes in his own life. As we sat side by side a wonderful heart-to-heart transaction occurred. I said to myself, "If Don wants to follow Jesus, so do I." What Don was modeling for me was that if you want to have a deep impact upon others you must get close to them. Only in retrospect did I realize that Don was modeling Jesus' method of ministry.

THE CALLING OF THE TWELVE

A moment of strategic importance occurred approximately a year into Jesus' public ministry. Luke signals this as a critical turning point by highlighting that Jesus held an all night prayer vigil on the eve of naming his twelve disciples. We know that Jesus had gathered an unknown number of disciples including Peter, James and John, as well as Levi (Matthew) the tax collector. From this larger entourage Jesus would choose his inner circle. "One of those days Jesus went out to a mountainside to pray, and spent the night praying to God. When morning came, he called his disciples to him and chose twelve of them, whom he also designated apostles" (Luke 6:12-13). If we could have listened in to Jesus' prayer that night, what might we have heard? My guess is that Jesus was quite aware that he was dealing with raw material. For example, upon meeting Peter, Jesus visualized his transformation. "'You are Simon son of John. You will be called Cephas' (which, when translated, is Peter [meaning rock])" (John 1:42). That was certainly not where Peter started, but it was where he ended under Jesus' shaping influence. These twelve ordinary men were being prepared to accept the responsibility to carry on the mission of Jesus after he returned to his Father.

What were some of the strategic reasons for Jesus focusing the bulk of his ministry on these twelve? Of the many reasons we could mention, two stand out:

- Internalization: In order for Jesus to transfer his message, manner, and mission, it required deep relational investment.

- Multiplication: Jesus reproduced his life in a few, as a model for what they would do for future generations.

INTERNALIZATION

Jesus staked the entirety of his ongoing mission to the world on the Twelve. He knew that disciples could not be made in crowds. As powerful as Jesus' teaching certainly was, it required very little to be a part of an audience. It is only as we come out of the crowd and identify ourselves with Jesus that we start the journey of discipleship.

Jesus prioritized personal relationship as the basis for internalizing his message, manner and mission in them. A good way to understand the nature of this relationship is to contrast it with the often-used church program approach to making disciples.

We are mistaken if we think that programs make disciples. We don't have the patience required for relationships, so we opt for the microwave approach since it is easier to have people walk through a set curriculum over a defined number of weeks. But once people have "graduated" from the program by completing all its requirements, we have a false sense of accomplishment. Jesus prioritized real life relationship but we substitute a system. What is the difference between a program and the relational approach?

Discipling relationships are marked by intimacy, whereas programs focus on information. Alicia Britt Chole captures Jesus' model of relational investment calling it "purposeful proximity." She says, "How easy it is to substitute informing people for investing in people, to confuse organizing people with actually discipling people. Life is not the offspring of program or paper. Life is the offspring of life."[3] The truth of Scripture comes alive when we can see it lived out through others. Don's life had an impact on me because he showed me how Scripture actually shaped his character. Programs are more concerned about information transfer. Discipling is lived truth. True knowledge is experiential, all the rest is just information.

Discipling relationships involve full, mutual participation, whereas programs rely on one or a few to do for the many. In a discipling relationship the partners equally share responsibility for preparation, self-disclosure and an agenda of life-change. This is not about one person being the insightful teacher, whereas the others are the learners. Certainly maturity levels will vary, but the basic assumption is that in the give and take, the one who is the teacher and the one who is the learner can vary from moment to moment. On the other hand, programs tend to rely on the expert who is delivering the content and the participants who are consumers of their preparation. The classic setting for this is preaching. The congregation is a passive audience, whereas the preacher is the one who has done all the work. To the extent that little is required of the hearer, transformation will be limited. I do believe in preaching but would not rely on it as the primary context to shape the character of a disciple. Preaching creates the motivation and then the need for making disciples, but not the environment. Even Jesus did not rely on his preaching or teaching to make disciples.

Discipling relationships are customized to the unique growth needs of the individuals, whereas programs emphasize synchronization and regimentation. Discipling relationships necessarily vary in length of time because no two people grow at the same speed. The uniqueness of each individual is front and center. Each person has a unique family history, personal challenges, internal battles, emotional makeup, spiritual journey and learning style. If transformation is to occur, all of these factors need to be considered. This can happen only to the extent that each person is known. A set program that requires the participants to walk in lockstep and be at the same place at the same time is akin to a production line. That kind of program discounts our humanity and individuality.

Discipling relationships focus accountability around life-change, whereas programs focus accountability around content. Growth into Christlikeness is the ultimate goal. The accountability in programs tends to be easily measurable, observable behaviors such as Scripture memory, completing the required weekly reading or filling in the blanks of the workbook. In a discipling relationship the accountability focuses on learning to obey Jesus' commands (Matthew 28:20). For example, there is a huge difference between knowing that Jesus taught us to love our enemies, and actually loving our enemies. Discipling relationships are centered on incorporating the life of Jesus in all we are in the context of all that we do.

Leroy Eims sums up Jesus' means for internalizing his message, manner and mission: "Disciples cannot be mass produced. We cannot drop people into a program and see disciples emerge at the end of a production line. It takes time to make disciples. It takes individual personal attention."[4]

MULTIPLICATION

The second reason for Jesus focusing on a few was *multiplication*. Since Jesus spent a considerable amount of time with just twelve people, one might conclude that he was unconcerned about the multitudes. Yet the opposite was true. He was so concerned that the crowds were "sheep without a shepherd" (Matthew 9:36) that he focused on multiplying more shepherds. In other words, Jesus had enough vision to think small. We are Christians in the twenty-first century because Jesus focused on a few. That's vision!

Jesus lived with a sense of urgency, an internal timetable, because he knew the sand was slipping through the hourglass. His divine appointment with the cross was approximately three and half years after the launch of his public ministry, just enough time to get his disciples ready to carry on after he was safely back home.

Just prior to Jesus' divine appointment with the cross, he uttered these most unusual words in his final prayer for his followers, "I have brought you glory on earth by finishing the work you gave me to do" (John 17:4). How is that possible? This was before Jesus uttered, "It is finished" from the cross. Yet there was another sense in which his work was done. He had poured his life into his disciples. *They* were his work. In God's perfect timing, just as Jesus' redemptive work on the cross was finished, so now his disciples were ready to carry on the mission to make disciples of all nations.

At a workshop, an elderly pastor spontaneously shared about his passion for discipling men. He had been at it for just three years. He started with one man; then they each worked with two others and from these six they each found two others. Now they were up to eighteen. In these three years they had grown into a dedicated band who were qualified to do the work of ministry. This pastor said that in his thirty-five years of ministry it was the most rewarding, fulfilling and exciting thing he had ever done.

APPLYING JESUS' MODEL OF DISCIPLEMAKING

What then are the implications of Jesus' model for us? How do we translate this into living as disciples today?

Make a decision to come out of the crowd and identify yourself with Jesus. The first step Jesus' disciples had to make was a willingness to be seen with Jesus as a part of his traveling band. Of course, this would become costly. At the time of Jesus' trial, Peter was identified by a servant girl as a follower: "You also were with that Nazarene, Jesus" (Mark 14:67). Peter denied knowing Jesus, failing this test. However, Jesus restored Peter after his resurrection, commissioning him to share the good news to the ends of the earth. And then when the Holy Spirit arrived, nothing could stop Peter. He was "all in."

The church today has been compared to a football game. There are fifty thousand people in the stands in desperate need of exercise, watching twenty-two people on the field in desperate need of rest. It is time to get out of crowd and onto the playing field.

Root yourself into the life of a small group whose expressed intent is to live as followers of Jesus in all dimensions of life. The point here is that there is no such thing as solo discipleship. Show me someone who says they don't need the encouragement and accountability of other believers and I will show you someone who has massive blind spots and is most likely not living a focused and consistent life in Christ. We all need "base" communities. These base communities are the places where our lives are consistently brought up next to the plumb line of biblical truth. It is from these base communities we are sent into all the various dimensions of life (i.e., family, work, church, relationships, thought life, finances, etc.).

Disciples of Jesus take a long-term perspective. In contrast to our short-term attention spans, we engage in discipling relationships as a lifestyle: this is the way we live together. Discipleship is not a program that begins in the fall and ends in the spring. It is not a curriculum you master and then ask, What's next? It is a relational life with other followers.

Make a commitment to become a multiplier. Integral to being a disciple of Jesus is to assume the responsibility of walking alongside others in order to help them grow in Christ so that they too can become multipliers. We often limit our understanding of growing to maturity in Christ to our own personal growth process. We become end-users of the resources that the church provides through preaching, classes, small groups, etc. When we understand what it means to be on the road to maturity in Christ, we are able to assist others in their discipleship as well.

What is our legacy? In God's value system our legacy is the people we have influenced to be Christ followers. I am Don's legacy. I am grateful that there are many who credit me as a primary influence in their life. This is our joy.

I am a sucker for emotional, tear-jerker movies. *Mr. Holland's Opus* is the story of a high school music teacher whose lifelong ambition was to make his mark by composing the great American symphony. Instead, he ended up with a career trying to teach high school students to appreciate music. After some failed attempts, he reshaped his pedagogy to see music through the eyes of his students. The students caught his vision but due to financial constraints, eventually Mr. Holland's position is eliminated.

The day he returns to clean out his office he hears rumblings in the auditorium. He opens the doors to a full auditorium with musicians on stage ready to play. In shock he exclaims, "What is this? What is going on?" There are his students, whose lives have been transformed, reflecting the impact of his thirty years of investment. Their response: "We are your symphony, Mr. Holland. We are the melody, the notes, the music you wrote. We are the symphony of your life."

In much the same way, our lives are to be a reflection of both the message and the method of Jesus' ministry.

Reading Study Guide

1. When you reflect on the story of Don's influence, is there someone who has influenced your motivation to be a follower of Jesus? What qualities in that person touched you?

2. Summarize your understanding of the two strategic reasons (*internalization* and *multiplication*) for Jesus' investment in a few.

3. What is the difference between a program and a relationship?

4. Why is relationship key to disciplemaking?

5. How did Jesus demonstrate his commitment to multiplication of disciples and leaders?

6. What does it mean for you to come out of the crowd and onto the path of following Jesus?

7. Why is belonging to and engaging with a small group so vital to your discipleship?

8. Can you see yourself getting to the point of assisting others in their growth in Christ? Why or why not?

---

[1]Greg Ogden, *Discipleship Essentials: A Guide to Building Your Life in Christ* (Downers Grove, IL: InterVarsity Press, 2007), 17.

[2]This quote was spoken at a seminar by Charles Miller, then Youth Pastor at Lake Avenue Congregational Church in Pasadena, CA.

[3]Alicia Britt Chole, "Purposeful Promixity—Jesus' Model of Mentoring," *Enrichment Journal* online, http://enrichmentjournal.ag.org/200102/062_proximity.cfm.

[4]Leroy Eims, *The Lost Art of Disciple Making* (Colorado Springs, CO: NavPress, 1978), 45.

7 / Transformation
Get Real and Find Freedom

LOOKING AHEAD

CORE TRUTH VERSE: "A cord of three strands is not quickly broken."
(Ecclesiastes 4:12)
BIBLE STUDY: Mark 10:35-45
READING: Living in the Hothouse of the Holy Spirit

 ## Core Truth

What are the necessary conditions to create an atmosphere of growth?

Since becoming a disciple of Jesus is fundamentally a relational process, disciples need to continually interweave their lives with others. An atmosphere of growth happens when these two conditions are present: (1) transparent trust is fostered through non-judgmental acceptance; and (2) the truth of God's Word is embraced and applied to all dimensions of life. These two conditions find their optimal expression in small groups of 3-4 people meeting regularly.

- What key thoughts from the Core Truth stand out to you and why?

- What questions or issues does the Core Truth raise for you?

Inductive Bible Study Guide

In walking with his band of disciples, Jesus was presented with teachable moments. James and John approached Jesus on the sly, out of earshot of the other ten apostles, with a request. Jesus uses this opportunity to teach them about the kind of relationships that build true community. *Read Mark 10:35-45.*

1. What is it that James and John want Jesus to do for them? (vv. 35-37)

   What is the underlying value that motivates this request?

2. How does Jesus respond to their request? (vv. 38-40)

3. How might this request of James and John undermine the trust among the Twelve?

4. What was the view of power and greatness in the culture of Jesus' day? (v. 42)

5. What alternative view of power and greatness does Jesus say should mark the relationships of his followers? (vv. 43-44)

6. What might it actually look like for Jesus' followers to demonstrate servanthood?

7. How is Jesus himself a model for this approach? (v. 45)

8. In what practical ways can a servant's attitude be expressed to each other in your group?

👓 Reading: Living in the Hothouse of the Holy Spirit

A number of years ago my wife and I had the privilege of a two-week vacation in Alaska in early July. During the summer months in Alaska, it is remarkable how rapidly things grow. We observed thousand pound pumpkins, daffodils the size of dinner plates and zucchini squash the length of baseball bats. What was it that made for this accelerated growth? From mid-May to the end of August the sun barely sets; Alaska becomes a "hothouse."

This has become for me a helpful image to describe what I have experienced in small groups of three or four (hereafter referred to as *micro groups*). Ever since I stumbled on my first group of three and was taken by its life-giving dynamic, I have been reflecting on the conditions for accelerated maturity in Christ: the "hothouse" effect.

What creates this kind of climatic condition for rapid growth as Christ followers? Two things: *transparent trust* and *the truth of God's Word*. When we open our hearts in transparent trust to each other around the truth of God's Word in community, we find ourselves in the Holy Spirit's hothouse of transformation.

OPEN OUR HEARTS IN TRANSPARENT TRUST

Micro groups are all about creating a relational setting marked by transparent trust. A woman was looking for partners with which to share her life. In her invitation to others to join her, she described transparent trust like this: "I am looking for people I can trust the big things with, mostly my dreams and my failures. A place filled with love and trust, not comparison or judgment."

Why is transparent trust a key ingredient for accelerated growth? Here is the guiding principle: *The extent to which we are willing to reveal to others those areas of life that need God's transforming touch is the extent to which we are inviting the Holy Spirit to make us new.* In other words, our willingness to be real with each other on a horizontal level is our pledge to God on the vertical level that we are truly serious about becoming all the Lord intends us to be.

I can hear the objections: Why do I need to reveal myself to others? God already knows all that there is know about the state of my heart. But this should give us pause. The prophet Jeremiah diagnoses the state of the human heart in the starkest terms: "The heart is deceitful above all things and beyond cure. Who can understand it?" (Jeremiah 17:9). Though there is no foolproof way to remain in the truth, a commitment to accountable relationship is one major step. The apostle John connects our ability to remain in truth and light to our relationships with each other: "If we claim to have fellowship with him and yet walk in the darkness, we lie and do not live out the truth. But if we walk in the light, as he is in the light, we have fellowship with one another, and the blood of Jesus, his Son, purifies us from all sin" (1 John 1:6-7).

Transparency in our relationships will require a trustworthy environment. Trustworthy. What an interesting word: *worthy of trust*. Trust is not a given, it is something that must be earned. An often-heard complaint by teenagers to their parents is, "You don't trust me!" If parents were honest, their reply might be something like, "You are darn right. I will trust you as soon as you demonstrate that I can trust you!" But how can we build trust?

Partners should not have to fear that their shared secret or even personal shame will come back to them through some other source outside the group because *trust keeps confidences*. The rule of thumb is that what is shared in the group stays in the group.

We will share with each other to the extent that we feel we are heard, so *trust listens*. Will our partners seek to know more? Will they stay with us, or will they deflect off to their own story and stifle self-revelation?

We come together as broken people so *trust is rooted in humility*. The humble have no pretense about their capacity for sin. There is nothing that surprises God about us, nor should there be about each other. Trust is unshockable.

What are some of stages or layers of trust development that we go through to get us to relational transparency? We can compare growing a trustworthy environment to wading into deeper waters together. Each successive stage signifies the rising tide.

Affirmation through encouragement (sticking our toe in the water). When a micro group first convenes, anxiety marks the beginning of the journey together. We are asking ourselves questions such as, Will I like my partners? Will they be safe to be around? Will they take an interest in my life? So we begin by sticking our toe in the water to take its temperature.

Trust grows when we experience those in the group as our cheer-leaders. This truth came home to me one Sunday just prior to worship. As I was leaving the restroom I found myself standing next to one of our worship leaders. I thought to myself, I rarely have the opportunity to express my appreciation to Chris for what he means to the quality of our worship life. So I said, "Chris, I just want to take this moment to thank you for the way you bring us into the presence of Christ. You truly are a gift to me and to so many others." What caught me off-guard was the intensity of his response. You would have thought that I had told him he had won a million dollars in the lottery. He ex-claimed, "Thank you *so* much! I hardly ever hear that." The world does a lot better job of beating us up than building us up.

Trust is built on the foundation of mutual encouragement. If this is our experience we are prepared to wade in more deeply.

Sharing life's difficulties (water up to our waist). If you are to-gether for at least a year, some quality of life-threatening experience will happen to one or more of the members of the group. This is truly the opportunity to come alongside and shoulder one another's afflictions. Paul wrote to struggling Thessalonians, "Night and day we pray most earnestly that we may see you again and supply what is lacking in your faith" (1 Thessalonians 3:10). There are truly times when we have to lean on the strength and confidence of one another's faith to make it through what life can throw at us.

I have been in the trenches with men with long-term unem-ployment, shaky marriages, runaway children, immanent home foreclosures, various kinds of addictions, life-threatening illnesses, major changes in life vocations, etc. Paul instructs us, "Carry each other's burdens, and in this way you will fulfill the law of Christ" (Galatians 6:2). When we have developed such a bond with each other that another's concern becomes our own, we are in the deeper waters together. It is a rare week that I don't leave my micro group with the sentiment, "What a privilege it was to be with these men today. Where else would we be able to share the weights we unloaded!"

***Listen deeply for God's direction** (water up to our shoulders).* Nothing builds trust like deep listening. Think of those who have a reputation in your life of being good listeners. When you are with them, they seem to be riveted on your story. They don't just ask the perfunctory question to make it seem like they are interested in you then go on to talk about themselves. No, they eagerly pursue you with one insightful question after another. They really want to know what is happening in your life. They have the uncanny ability to make you feel like you are the only person on the planet that matters in that moment.

What if we paid attention to each other like that in our groups? In particular, we want to listen for the way God is moving in our partners' lives. Listening is a gift we give when someone is attempting to discern God's direction in their life. Dave had spent thirty-two years in the insurance business. In fact, our micro group met around the conference room table in his insurance office. During our time together, Dave began to sense that the Lord was leading him in a radical new direction. He had built up a solid portfolio and was highly regarded in the insurance world. Life was comfortable, but something was stirring. We regularly set aside time to listen to Dave in an attempt to help him get in touch with what was being birthed in him. In a sense we became spiritual midwives, watching the baby mature to the place where he gave up his safe career and joined an organization that coaches Christian CEOs to live out their discipleship in the business world. Dave credits the micro group as his listening post where he could test and discern God's voice in his life.

When you get this involved in the depth of each other's lives, you might as well get in over your head.

Mutual confession (water over our heads). The deep water of transparent trust is mutual confession of our sin. In my experience very few believers have either the regular habit or a safe place to reveal to others what lurks in the recesses of our hearts. But until we get to the point where we can articulate to others those things that have a hold on us, we live under the tyranny of our own darkness. James admonishes us, "Confess your sins to each other and pray for each other so that you may be healed" (James 5:16). Another way to translate this is, "Confess your sins . . . so that you can live together whole and healed" (*The Message*). When we bring our guilt and shame into the light of trusted, non-condemning brothers and sisters, it has a liberating effect. Sin finds strength in the darkness, but weakens in the light.

Unfortunately, most of us avoid confession, mistakenly assuming that revealing our sins will push others away. But Deitrich Bonhoeffer corrects this thinking as he addresses the power of confession:

> In confession the break-through to community takes place. Sin demands to have a man by himself. It withdraws him from the community. The more isolated a person is, the more destructive will be the power of sin over him, and the more deeply he becomes involved in it, the more disastrous is his isolation. . . . In confession the light of the Gospel breaks into the darkness and seclusion of the heart. . . . Since the confession of sin is made in the presence of a Christian brother, the last stronghold of self-justification is abandoned.[1]

Transparent trust expresses our deepest desire to be laid bare so that God can have his way with us. King David expresses this deep trust in God when he says,

Search me, God, and know my heart;
  test me and know my anxious thoughts.
See if there is any offensive way in me,
  and lead me in the way everlasting. (Psalm 139:23-24)

AROUND THE TRUTH OF GOD'S WORD

The second climatic condition necessary to produce the hothouse of
the Holy Spirit is the application of the truth of God's Word in a relational environment. You might be wondering why the truth of God's
Word is the second condition. Isn't Scripture primary? It is, but it
needs a context in which it can be processed. Bible studies are a staple
in most churches, but there appears to be limited life-transformation
through these groups. So many Bible studies seem to focus on in-
creased information without life application.

The application of Word to life is what I call *truth in community*.
We bring our open lives to the Word of God and allow it to do its
work in us as we share our stories and journey together. In his letter
to Timothy, Paul details the purpose of God's word: "All Scripture is
God-breathed and is useful for teaching, rebuking, correcting and
training in righteousness" (2 Timothy 3:16).

Teaching can be translated as "doctrine," which is simply a
statement of God's truth. In our day in particular, we need to cover
truth in a systematic way to capture the big picture of the Christian
life. Following the completion of one my micro groups, one of the
partners in the group approached me and said, "I have a confession
to make. When you asked me to be in the group, I didn't think I had
that much to learn. After all I had been studying Scripture my
whole life, having been raised in the home of a pastor where the
Bible was central. But I discovered that as I explored the faith in a
systematic and sequential fashion, my understanding was much
like a mosaic. There were entire sections of missing pieces. I now

have a much more comprehensive picture how the Christian faith makes sense of it all."

A lack of integration of faith and life seems to be the norm rather than the exception. Throughout our Christian journey it is as if we have accumulated puzzle pieces and tossed them into a box. We accrue bits and pieces of truth through sermons, reading, devotional resources, wisdom from fellow believers, Bible studies, etc. These puzzle pieces are all jumbled together but not assembled into a comprehensive whole. A sequential, layer upon layer discipleship curriculum can create a holistic picture of God's view of reality.[2]

Two of the other purposes of Scripture are *rebuking* and *correcting*. Rebuking involves a reproof or reprimand. For example, Paul writes, "Do not let any unwholesome talk come out of your mouths" (Ephesians 4:29). As you read this word perhaps the Holy Spirit brings to mind how you used sarcasm to cut another down while drawing attention to yourself. The Word exposes, and sometimes it feels like a dagger to the heart. So you share this with your partners in confession. They help you back onto right path through correction. This might entail going to the person you harmed and asking for forgiveness.

THE POWER OF A MICRO GROUP

What is the biblical foundation for these groups of transparent trust? Ecclesiastes touts the protection and strength that comes from intertwined lives:

> By yourself you're unprotected.
> With a friend you can face the worst.
> Can you round up a third?
> A three-stranded rope isn't easily snapped.
> (Ecclesiastes 4:12 *The Message*)

Jesus modeled this same dynamic in his relationship with Peter, James and John. On three special occasions—at the raising of Jairus's daughter, on the Mount of Transfiguration and in the Garden of Gethsemane just prior to the cross (Mark 5:37; 9:2; 14:33)—we learn that these three were singled out. Jesus invited these three into the circle dance of love.

A growing disciple of Jesus will adopt a lifestyle of investment with two to three others. The optimum setting to integrate transparent trust with the application of God's Word is a micro group. Its small size allows each person to be known as the unique individual they are. Each person's story can be heard. Everyone has the opportunity to share their insights into Scripture and where truth intersects life. These micro groups serve as the hothouses that accelerate our growth in Christ. Make it your lifelong habit.

Reading Study Guide

1. What is the hothouse effect?

2. How would you describe the quality of transparent trust? Why is it vital for accelerated growth?

3. What are the elements that build trust?

4. Share a personal anecdote that describes each of the four stages of trust:

- encouragement through affirmation:

- sharing life's difficulties:

- listening deeply for God's direction:

- mutual confession:

5. Why is it vital to explore God's Word in the context of transparent trust?

6. In what way has your understanding of God and Scripture been like a jumble of puzzle pieces? What steps can you take to remedy this?

7. How do you see a micro group fitting into your priorities going forward?

---

[1]Dietrich Bonhoeffer, *Life Together* (Harper & Row: New York, 1954), 112.
[2]*Discipleship Essentials*, the curriculum I have written, was created in order to give a holistic, sequential picture of the core foundations of a disciple's life.

8 / The Jesus Promise

I Am with You Always

LOOKING AHEAD

CORE TRUTH VERSE: "And surely I am with you always, to the very end of the age." (Matthew 28:20)
BIBLE STUDY: John 14:15-27
READING: Fear Not, I Am with You Always

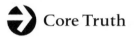 Core Truth

What does Jesus' promise to those engaged in his disciple-making mission?

Jesus began his call to make disciples with the full backing of his authority and concludes the call with the assurance to be with us always. Jesus' promise to be our ever-present companion is designed to address our fears in the face of opposition. Jesus is saying essentially, "Fear not! For with my backing you will be equipped to carry out my mission."

- What key thoughts from the Core Truth stand out to you and why?

- What questions or issues does the Core Truth raise for you?

Inductive Bible Study

During Jesus' final gathering with his disciples prior to the cross, he sent shockwaves of abandonment through them when he said, "Where I am going, you cannot come" (John 13:33). Yet Jesus assured them that he would come to them and remain with them in a way that exceeds his physical presence by sending an "advocate": the Holy Spirit. *Read John 14:15-27.*

1. Jesus told the disciples that the Father would give them "another advocate" (v. 16). If the Holy Spirit is *another* advocate, what role will the Spirit play in the lives of the disciples? What does this imply about the Spirit's relationship to Jesus?

2. How long will the Holy Spirit (advocate) be with them? Where will the Holy Spirit dwell? (vv. 16-17)

3. Jesus said, "I will not leave you as orphans" (v. 18). Why might Jesus have used the term "orphans" to reassure his disciples? What fears was he addressing?

4. What three things will the disciples realize (know by experience), when the Holy Spirit comes? (v. 20)

5. How might these realizations comfort the disciples?

6. As you look at verse 27, what is the nature of the peace that Jesus gives to comfort their troubled hearts?

7. As a follower of Christ, what circumstances might you find yourself in where you are troubled or afraid? Intercede for one another, praying for peace in those circumstances.

Reading: Fear Not, I Am with You Always

Fear.

I often wonder if fear is not the strongest of human emotions. Scripture says that perfect love casts out fear, yet fear often seems to triumph. It is the great interrupter. The prophet Elijah could not have had a more dramatic demonstration of the power of God with his triumph over the prophets of Baal. But no sooner had God rained down fire from heaven than we see Elijah fleeing in fear. Queen Jezebel, King Ahab's wife, had taken a contract out on Elijah's head. "I have had enough, LORD," Elijah cried out as he fled to the wilderness, "Take my life" (1 Kings 19:4). One moment Elijah was full of faith taunting the prophets of Baal, and the next moment he was full of fear. Life had drained from him.

William Paul Young's novel *The Shack* became a surprising best-seller in part because it spoke to this deep universal experience of fear. The story is about Mack, a father devastated by the brutal murder of his daughter, Missy. Mack's ensuing anger and fear left him imprisoned in what he calls "The Great Sadness." Then he received a strange invitation from Papa (God the Father) to meet him back at the scene of his daughter's murder, the shack. The story that ensues portrays the triune God orchestrating Mack's redemption.

In a dialogue with the Holy Spirit, Mack asks, "Why do I have so much fear in my life?" The Spirit answered,

> Because you don't believe. You don't believe we [the Father, Son, and Holy Spirit] love you. The person who lives by their fears will not find freedom in my love. . . . To the degree that those fears have a place in your life, you neither believe I am good nor know how deep in your heart that I love you. You can sing about it; you can talk about it, but you don't know it.[1]

Fear can be the biggest obstacle to our experience of the goodness and love of God.

This is why Jesus targets our fear when he offers this wondrous promise: "And surely I am with you always, to the very end of the age" (Matthew 28:20). The phrases "I am with you" and "I will be with you" appear throughout Scripture, most often addressing fear evoked due to God's call. His followers were called to accomplish things that humans could not possibly pull off on their own; they were doomed to failure unless the Lord was the One who did these things through them.

How does God address the fears of his called servants?

To the patriarch Isaac, the son of Abraham, the Lord said, "Do not be afraid, for I am with you; I will bless you and will increase the number of your descendants for the sake of my servant Abraham" (Genesis 26:24).

In the wilderness, the Lord informed Moses of his call to release God's people from Pharaoh's captivity. Moses rightfully responded, "Who am I that I should go?" But the Lord reassured him, "I will be with you" (Exodus 3:11-12).

When Jeremiah was called to be a prophet, he objected on the grounds that he was too young and inexperienced. But the Lord replied, "Do not be afraid . . . for I am with you and will rescue you" (Jeremiah 1:8).

And through the prophet Isaiah the Lord speaks to any overwhelming circumstance in our life when he says,

> So do not fear, for I am with you;
>> do not be dismayed, for I am your God.
> I will strengthen you and help you;
>> I will uphold you with my righteous right hand.
>> (Isaiah 41:10)

The number one command in Scripture, some 365 references, is some form of "Do not be afraid."

At this point you might have a number of questions about what it means to be a follower of Jesus—questions that are expressions of your fears:

FEAR OF COMMITMENT: *WHAT WILL IT COST ME TO FOLLOW JESUS?*

Before Elijah ran in fear, he was full of faith. In front of the gathered nation of Israel, Elijah drew a line in the sand and posed a challenge, "How long will you waver between two opinions? If the LORD is God, follow him; but if Baal is God, follow him" (1 Kings 18:21). Elijah challenged them to depart from the no man's land of doubt and indecision. To doubt is to waver between belief and unbelief. But Elijah points to the fact that at some point we must choose. Commit. But at what cost?

In his book *Seeking Allah, Finding Jesus*, Nabeel Qureshi tells of the price a devout Muslim must pay to change his loyalty to Christ. Nabeel was raised in the United States by loving and highly respected parents who taught him to love Islam. His life was defined by his Islamic faith interwoven within a tight-knit subculture. In response to his Christian peers during his high school years, he was able to thwart their witnessing attempts by raising questions they were unable to answer. But things changed when he went off to college. During his freshman year he met David, a follower of Christ, who not only had a joyful and loving demeanor, but knew what he believed and why.

They became fast friends throughout their college years as members of the debate team. David kept raising issues for Nabeel to examine, such as comparing Muhammad with Jesus, the reliability of the Koran versus Scripture, the evidence for the resurrection of Jesus, etc. Nabeel pursued these challenges because he was convinced that in doing so he would prove his Islamic faith was on solid ground and superior to Christianity. What he increasingly discovered was the opposite. Nabeel finally became convinced both through reason and a series of dreams that he must make a commitment to Christ.

But Nabeel knew that to make Christ his Lord would mean disappointing the most revered and beloved people in his life: his parents. Nabeel was forced to choose between two loves: his love of God and his love for his parents. The cost of following Christ is captured in the dedication to his book:

Ammi and Abba (Mom and Dad), your undying love for me even when you feel I have sinned against you is second only to God's love for His children. I pray you will one day realize His love is truly unconditional, that He has offered forgiveness to us all. On that day, I pray that you would accept redemption, so we might be a family once again. I love you with all my heart.[2]

At a great cost—the loss of relationship with his parents—Nabeel took up Elijah's challenge to choose and commit.

Jesus' reassuring conclusion to the Great Commission is designed to address this cost of commitment. Whatever the cost, we have the greatest of all compensations: Jesus' eternal and abiding presence. Yes, there is a price to pay, but the price of noncommitment is greater if you miss out on Jesus.

FEAR FROM SELF-DOUBT: *DO I HAVE WHAT IT TAKES?*

This was Moses' conundrum. When Moses looked at what God was asking him to do, and the necessary skills, he wanted no part of it. Moses was recruited by the Lord to go before the most formidable political ruler of his day, the Pharaoh of Egypt, and demand that his work force be reduced by a few million people. Moses' fear, doubt and insecurities seem reasonable in those circumstances. So Moses issued a series of questions and objections to God.

First, he wanted to know what to tell the Israelites when they asked who sent him. God gave his covenant name when he said to Moses, "I AM WHO I AM. . . . Say to the Israelites: 'I AM has sent me to you'" (Exodus 3:14). But Moses was not convinced: "What if they do not believe me or listen to me and say, 'The LORD did not appear to you'?" (Exodus 4:1). In response, the Lord performed a series of miracles through Moses: a staff turned into a snake and then back to a staff, Moses' hand became leprous and then was healed, and water from the Nile turned into blood. Moses then issued his final objection in order to get out of this call, "Lord, I have never been eloquent" (Exodus 4:10), to which the Lord promised to help Moses speak and teach him what to say. Finally, Moses went for the opt-out clause, "Please send someone else" (Exodus 4:13). At that point the Lord lost his patience with all these objections, but did not relent. He simply provided Aaron, Moses' brother, to be his mouthpiece.

Later when Joshua was commissioned as Moses' successor, the Lord said, "Be strong and courageous, for . . . I myself will be with you" (Deuteronomy 31:23). The Lord promises his followers that if he has called them to a particular task, he will provide what is needed to carry that out. So when Jesus say, "I am with you," he means, "I will accomplish my purposes through you."

To experience God's provision will require we face up to and walk into our fears. Nelson Mandela, like few others, had the moral authority to stand behind his words: "I learned that courage was not the absence of fear, but the triumph over it. The brave man is not he who does not feel afraid, but he who conquers that fear."[3] Personally, as I look back on my life, the Lord has only been able to grow me when I did not allow fear to deter me. When I was first asked to teach fellow pastors at the doctoral level, I was terrified to stand up in front of my peers—many of whom were older than me. During my first weeklong intensive course, I barely slept. But the Lord walked with me into my fears. He keeps elevating us to higher platforms of risk because this is the way he expands what he can do through us.

FEAR OF RISK: *WHAT IF I GET IN OVER MY HEAD?*

As long as we remain in the safe confines of the comfortable, minimal growth will occur. Biblical faith compels us to take risks. Jesus promised that he would meet us on the stretch. It is popular wisdom that God will not give us more than we can handle. More accurately God promises to be with us in whatever situation that risky faith has led us into. Pastor John Ortberg tells the story of going parasailing with his then ten-year-old son. The boat driver said they had the option of ascending to 400, 600 or 800 feet. As they talked it over, John's son remarked that the whole thing felt a bit frightening. But then he spoke insight beyond his years. "I'm gonna go up 800 feet. I might be scared when I go up there at first. But I'm going to do it because the ride only lasts a few minutes. But once it's over, I'll have it forever."[4] In the grand scheme of things, this life only lasts for "a few minutes." But Jesus says, "Go for it. I am with you all the way."

FEAR OF ABANDONMENT: *WILL I BE ALONE?*

Abandonment is perhaps is the greatest of human fears. In fact, Eve was created for Adam because the Lord declared that it wasn't good for Adam to be alone (Genesis 2:18). We think of Tom Hanks in the film *Cast Away*. Stranded on an uninhabited island, his character needed to create a personage out of a volleyball he named Wilson to maintain his sanity. The severest punishment prisoners can receive is to put them in solitary confinement for long periods of time. Without others, we lose any sense of who we are.

Ultimately we will all face death alone. Yet Jesus not only spoke to this deepest fear, he took it on. In the moment when the guilt of our sin was placed upon Jesus, our substitute, he uttered these words: "My God, my God, why have you forsaken me?" (Matthew 27:46). None of us can comprehend the utter forsakenness that Jesus experienced in that moment. The One who lived in communion with his Father in open and transparent loving relationship was cut off. The religious leaders trumped up charges against him and taunted him at the foot of the cross: "He saved others . . . but he can't save himself!" (Matthew 27:42). Jesus was betrayed by Judas and denied by Peter. And on the cross, even his Father appeared to be absent, utterly silent. Whatever was happening between the Father and the Son in this singular redemptive moment, we know that Jesus at least felt deserted.

Why did Jesus put himself through this? So that we would never have to experience what he experienced. Now that we are on the resurrection side of the cross, Jesus promises that this will never happen to us. His abiding presence will never leave us or forsake us.

CONCLUSION

As we close these reflections on what it means to be a follower of Jesus, let's look at Jesus' closing promise one phrase at a time: "And surely I am with you always, to the very end of the age" (Matthew 28:20).

And surely I . . . Jesus emphatically puts himself forth as our major resource. He supplies the power to be a disciple.

. . . am with you . . . Jesus is our companion on this journey to follow him. He is enough.

. . . always, to the very end of the age. Not just the good days, or most days, or even the days we feel spiritually fit, but all our days he is *always* available.

Reading Study Guide

1. What makes fear such an overpowering and disruptive emotion?

2. How does the Holy Spirit address Mack's question as to why he has so much fear?

3. In what ways can you identify with the different ways that fear disrupts our trust and confidence in God?

4. What was the cost that Nabeel Qureshi had to pay to choose Jesus?

5. What might it cost you to be a fully devoted Christ follower?

6. What fear might the Lord be asking you to face or walk into with his full backing?

7. How does Jesus' forsakenness on the cross address the fear of abandonment?

8. As you consider what it means to be a devoted follower of Jesus, where do you need Jesus to speak peace into your life?

---

[1]Wm. Paul Young, *The Shack* (Windblown Media: Los Angeles, 2007), 142.
[2]Nabeel Qureshi, *Seeking Allah, Finding Jesus* (Grand Rapids: Zondervan, 2014).
[3]Nelson Mandela, *Long Walk to Freedom* (Little, Brown: New York, 1995), 622.
[4]John Ortberg, *If You Want to Walk on Water, You've Got to Get Out of the Boat* (Grand Rapids: Zondervan, 2001), 133.

Closing Challenge

Are You Ready to Be "All In"?

What are you committing to as a disciple of Jesus? Jesus' issued a sobering challenge to count the cost. Whether it is building a tower or preparing for battle, you must assess upfront if you have what it takes. Jesus was not a bait and switch kind of person. He didn't dangle shiny objects in front of people and then change the terms once people were in. From the beginning he laid it out there. Jesus said, "Whoever wants to be my disciple must deny themselves and take up their cross daily and follow me" (Luke 9:23).

Let's review in succinct fashion what we have learned that a follower of Jesus must consider:

- Disciples submit themselves to the authority of the One who has it all. Jesus calls the shots.

- Disciples shift their loyalty from the kingdoms of this world to the kingdom of God's beloved Son.

- Disciples are captured by a "go-spirit" that compels them to share the good news in word and deed, near and far.

- Disciples root their fundamental identity in the knowledge that they have been included in the circle love of the three-person God.

- Disciples enter into a life-long quest to adjust their lives in obedience to everything that Jesus commanded.

- Disciples root themselves in a community of fellow disciples in order to stay focused on being a faithful Christ follower.

- Disciples live in and reproduce the "hothouse" environment of transformation that leads to Christlikeness.

- Disciples can face the fear that they don't have what it takes, because Jesus has promised to give us his full backing. He will never leave us or forsake us.

A way to simplify the eight points above is to capture the life of a disciple under three headings:

Disciples join Jesus' life. A Christian is one who is "in Christ" and has "Christ in you." Jesus says of us that we are like branches attached to the vine from which life flows (John 15:1-8). The apostle Paul picks up on this agrarian image when he says, "For if we have been united with him in a death like his, we will certainly also be united with him in a resurrection like his" (Romans 6:5). The word *united* literally means "engrafted." We are like branches cut from another tree and then have been fused through the process of engrafting onto the true vine. It is only as we "remain," stay connected to the vine, that we have life. Life flows only in one direction: *from* the vine *to* the branches. The branches have no life in themselves apart from the vine. So a disciple is one who first and foremost understands that apart from him we can do nothing.

Disciples join Jesus' community. An important aspect of being engrafted is becoming an integral part of the body of Christ. We are saved into a new community in whom Jesus has invested his life. The image of the church as Christ's body is far more than a nice metaphor or word picture. Quite literally, Jesus continues to live out his life on earth through his people. Just as there is no life apart from our attachment to him, there is no discipleship apart from his community. One vital way we are connected to the body is to participate in a micro group whose members are seeking to become all that Jesus intended.

Disciples join Jesus' mission. Simply put, his mission is to make disciples. This means that we see our identity—all that we are and do: our vocation or calling as spouse, child, parent, occupation, volunteer, coach, homemaker, etc.—through the lens of being a disciple of Jesus. We answer the "Who are you?" question with "I am a follower of Jesus." Then as followers of Jesus, our mission is to make more and better disciples. This entails doing all that we can to be equipped for this mission.

So what will it be? Are you ready to make the commitment to see yourself first and foremost as one sitting at the feet of your mentor, Jesus?

Reading Study Guide

1. Read over slowly, multiple times the above profile of a disciple of Jesus. Can you honestly say, "Yes, that is what I want to become"? Are you all in?

2. If there is some hesitancy about throwing your lot in with Jesus, can you name what is holding you back?

3. What would you need to overcome that hesitancy?

4. If you are ready, write your own prayer of commitment. Tell Jesus what you want to do. Then share this commitment with others in your group.

The Essentials Set

Also by Greg Ogden

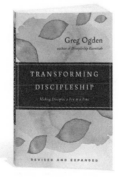

Global Discipleship Initiative (GDI) trains, supports, and releases pastors and Christian leaders to establish indigenous, multiplying, disciple-making networks of all God's people, both domestically and internationally.

GDI offers one-day **workshops** and ministry-based **coaching**, as well as more extensive **training** domestically.

For more information, go to globaldiscipleshipinitiative.org

or contact us directly:
Pastor Ralph Rittenhouse, president, ralph@globaldi.org
Dr. Greg Ogden, chairman of the board, greg@globaldi.org